FOLLOW FOR NOW, VOL. 2

Before you start to read this book, take this moment to think about making a donation to punctum books, an independent non-profit press,

@ https://punctumbooks.com/support/

If you're reading the e-book, you can click on the image below to go directly to our donations site. Any amount, no matter the size, is appreciated and will help us to keep our ship of fools afloat. Contributions from dedicated readers will also help us to keep our commons open and to cultivate new work that can't find a welcoming port elsewhere. Our adventure is not possible without your support.

Vive la Open Access.

Fig. 1. Hieronymus Bosch, *Ship of Fools* (1490–1500)

FOLLOW FOR NOW, VOL. 2. Copyright © 2021 by the editor and authors. This work carries a Creative Commons BY-NC-SA 4.0 International license, which means that you are free to copy and redistribute the material in any medium or format, and you may also remix, transform and build upon the material, as long as you clearly attribute the work to the authors (but not in a way that suggests the authors or punctum books endorses you and your work), you do not use this work for commercial gain in any form whatsoever, and that for any remixing and transformation, you distribute your rebuild under the same license. http://creativecommons.org/licenses/by-nc-sa/4.0/

First published in 2021 by punctum books, Earth, Milky Way.
https://punctumbooks.com

ISBN-13: 978-1-953035-80-6 (print)
ISBN-13: 978-1-953035-81-3 (ePDF)

DOI: 10.53288/0331.1.00

LCCN: 2021945292
Library of Congress Cataloging Data is available from the Library of Congress

Book Design: Vincent W.J. van Gerven Oei

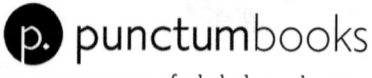

spontaneous acts of scholarly combustion

HIC SVNT MONSTRA

Roy Christopher, ed.

FOLLOW FOR NOW, Vol. 2
More Interviews with Friends and Heroes

to Cindy

Contents

Preface   13

MEDIA

Carla Nappi: Historical Friction   20
Kristen Gallerneaux: Unattended Consequences   34
Dominic Pettman: Human Matters   46
Rita Raley: Tactical Humanities   52
Jodi Dean: Of Crowds and Collectives   58
Gareth Branwyn: Borg Like Me   64
Ian Bogost: Worthwhile Dilemmas   72
Mark Dery: Nothing's Shocking   82
Brian Eno: Strange Overtones   90
Zizi Papacharissi: A Networked Self   98
Douglas Rushkoff: The User's Dilemma   104
danah boyd: Privacy = Context + Control   110
Dave Allen: Every Force Evolves a Form   114

HIP-HOP

Juice Aleem: Don't Be Afraid of the Dark   128
Labtekwon: Margin Walker   134
M. Sayyid: The Other Side   140
Shabazz Palaces: A New Refutation   146
dälek: Build and Destroy   152
Matthew Shipp: Heavy Meta   158

Tyler, The Creator: The Odd Future Is Now	164
Tricia Rose: Warrior Soul	170
Sean Price: Bless the M.I.C.	176
Rammellzee: The Wrath of the Math	180
Cadence Weapon: Check the Technique	186
El-P: Wake Up. Time to Die.	190
Sadat X: My Protocol Is Know-It-All	200

WRITING

Ytasha L. Womack: Dance to the Future	206
Bob Stephenson: Bit by Bit	216
Pat Cadigan: Eyes on the Skies	220
Mish Barber-Way: Flour Power	226
Chris Kraus: Wildly Contradictory	232
Simon Critchley: The Skull beneath the Skin	236
Clay Tarver: Gone Glimmering	242
Nick Harkaway: A Dynastic Succession of Trouble	248
Simon Reynolds: Erase and Start It Again	256
Malcolm Gladwell: Epidemic Proportions	264
William Gibson: The Co-Evolution of Humans and Machines	268

PREFACE

O Bother, Why Art Thou?

In the late aughts, I did a talk at several events and on several college campuses called "How to Do Stuff and Be Happy." The title was a joke, but the advice was real. It was a bunch of things I'd learned in the pursuit of various interests, mostly writing and publishing. Someone asked me recently why I bother to do any of the things I do. What follows emerged from an attempt to answer that question.

I started making zines in my teens. My friend Matt Bailie and I saw the first zine-review article in *Freestylin' Magazine* and decided we should make one ourselves. It was the spring of 1986. We were just about to start high school.

Ten years later I registered the domain name of the last long-running zine I'd been making, and *frontwheeldrive.com* became my first website. After a false start or two, I ran the site steadily from 1999 to 2008. Two other like-minded dudes, Tom Georgoulias and Brandon Pierce, and I did interviews and wrote reviews about media and science and culture and whatever. Somewhere in there, I self-published the best of those interviews as a book called *Follow for Now: Interviews with Friends and Heroes* (Well-Red Bear, 2007).

One wrongheaded move I made during my transition from skateboarding and music zines to heavy, heady websites was thinking that I needed to completely replace old interests with new ones. I had just become a reader of books and was wishing I'd been one all along, so it was out with the hip-hop and punk rock and skateboarding and in with the science and literature and media theory. Eventually I realized that if not for the one there wouldn't be the other. Music taught me how to do research. Who was on what record label, who used to be in what band with whom, who produced what, who was down with whom — these were the footnotes. I was already digging for sources, for citations. Skateboarding introduced me to art and determination and all of the music I love. Everything is research, and there's room for all of it.

For the decade after closing *frontwheeldrive.com,* I reluctantly moved everything over to a blog format under my own name, *roychristopher.com.* One of the things I had finally realized about strictly publishing interviews with other people is that the other people are the focus. That's exactly how that should be, but if you're trying to build your name as a writer, as I was, the interview format doesn't showcase your writing. Blogging, for what it's worth, does that. It's you and your words, and that's it.

I learned another minor lesson from simply the naming of a thing: as flimsy a front as it might be, if you run a publication, people will quote it, assuming you're giving them words worth quoting. They will proudly print, "she told Roy Christopher of *frontwheeldrive.com*..." If you're a nobody like me, they won't quote you if the website bears your name. They won't proudly print, "she told Roy Christopher of *roychristopher.com*...": a small lesson, but a lesson nonetheless.

Through two decades of doing these two websites, as well as all the zines and my magazine work that preceded them, I suppose I have managed to establish myself enough to be able to pitch ideas, write books, and do freelance writing here and there. One thing that differentiates my writing from some of my colleagues and peers is that I don't rely on it for my living. The truth is that, aside from a few years in the 1990s, I've just never been able to pay my bills as a writer. Hell, since then being a writer has cost me money! That's not a complaint, nor is it important.

What's important is that whether or not you rely on something to pay your bills changes the goals and the results of that something. For instance, I was interviewing a band last week. There is nothing unique about my interviewing a band. I've been doing it for a while. The difference is that if I'm interviewing a band, it's because I like them. I'm interested beyond the story I'm writing. That makes the way I do interviews different from when I would do them on assignment for money. It changes them so much that the bands I interview usually notice the difference.

I hope the same can be said for my writing in general. Dan Hancox at *The Guardian* (see?) described my recent book, *Dead Precedents,* as "written with the passion of a zine-publishing fan and the acuity of an academic." That's the kind of compliment you hope for, and it comes from pursuing a certain kind of goal.

One of the things I have found when teaching writing to others is that students have the most difficulty coming up with something to write about. More than any other part of the writing process, topic selection stumps them; more than the challenge of the initial blank page, or coming up with titles, thesis statements, headlines, leads, or anything else. I tell them to find something they already like, that they want to know more about and that they want to tell people about.

That impulse, that desire to tell others about something cool, is the core reason I do just about everything I do. It's the reason I'm a writer. It's the reason I'm a teacher. It's the reason I made zines. It's the reason I made websites. It's the reason I'm writing this right now.

No one can tell you "How to Do Stuff and Be Happy," but when you find that thing, that impulse, that thing you'll do anyway, you'll be on your way.

With all of that written, I am so very happy to have compiled a second volume of *Follow for Now*. As with the first one, I've tried to arrange these discussions in somewhat fluid categories. I often use the tagline "I marshal the middle between Mathers and McLuhan," which is of course intended to be cute and catchy, but it also sums up my research interests. On one side I am interested in figurative language use, specifically allusions in media. I have found these especially prevalent in hip-hop lyrics. On the other side, I am interested in technology and media theory. While I investigate these two areas separately, I have found the space where they overlap especially interesting. So, these three areas — Media, Hip-hop, and Writing — are the categories I used for the interviews in this volume. This arrangement is in the hope of helping you find the people you know and guiding you through the ones you don't. Every interview is date stamped. The introductions remain from the initial occasion the interviews were done, and a lot of these interviews took place just before their subjects went on to do the thing you know them for. Run the Jewels wasn't yet a group when I talked to El-P about his music. Malcolm Gladwell had only just written the first of his many bestsellers when we talked in 2002. The Tyler, the Creator interview is his first ever. He'd yet to record anything for a label when Tim Baker emailed him about an interview, and he'd yet to be interviewed by anyone in the media. Others have written and released many projects since these discussions. Since the hiatus during which we talked, Will Brooks has reformed dälek. Rammellzee and Sean Price have both since passed on.

Though most of these interviews were done since the last volume, not all of them were initially done with public consumption in mind. Many first appeared on *roychristopher.com*, but many were done purely for research and many of the questions come from personal curiosity rather than to serve an audience. You can think of those as raw files or addenda to the works discussed. Still other interviews collected here have never been published. Several were done specifically for this book and some just never made it off of various hard drives. I did some excavating in a few cases, including my previously mentioned interview with Malcolm Gladwell and Kodwo Eshun's 1996 discussion with William Gibson, the latter of which is published here for the first time anywhere.

I owe a huge thanks to all of the interviewees for gifting their time and many insights, without which, no interviews to collect, no book. Thank you all. Same goes to the other interviewers who let me print or reprint their discussions here: Alfie Bown, Timothy Baker, Chuck Galli, Steven Johnson, and Kodwo Eshun. And to the others who helped at various points: Alex Burns, Dave Tompkins, Bekah Zietz Flynn at Sub Pop, Wes Harden, Peter Agoston, Hector A. Silva, Charles Mudede, Donal Logue, Mike Ladd, Mark Lewman, Spike Jonze, and Hannah Liley at the Otilith Group.

I also have to thank the artists I got to draw the interviewee portraits throughout the book: Eleanor Purcell, Laura Persat (I told you I'd get you in the next one, Miss Laura!), and Josh Row. I did a few myself, but as you'll soon see, my scribbling cannot compare to the stunning work of these folks. Look them up and pay them to draw cool stuff for you.

I was privileged to work with Eileen A. Joy and Vincent W.J. van Gerven Oei at punctum books. I like to claim that I'm a good scholar but a bad academic. Punctum is all about the knowledge-spreading and discourse of the former but not so much the structures and strictures of the latter. Eileen and Vincent make sure the work stays not only rigorous and challenging but also accessible and open. You should go subscribe and support their work at punctum now.

As always, thanks to my partner Lily Brewer. I cannot even tell you.

MEDIA

1

CARLA NAPPI
Historical Friction

Interview by Roy Christopher
Illustration by Laura Persat
August 3, 2019

Being undecided is an undergraduate punchline, but it's also a strong postgraduate desire. As a scholar, wanting to exist outside or in between disciplines goes largely unrewarded in academia. Collaborating across many established boundaries, Carla Nappi is a historian in the broadest, most rebellious sense of the word. She is the Andrew W. Mellon Chair in the Department of History at the University of Pittsburgh where she runs the Center for Historical Pataphysics. Her academic and artistic practices include the history of China, Manchu studies, world history, translation, and writing, among other areas. As she puts it on her website, "I write about writing and read about reading and write about writing about reading and read about reading about writing." She and Dominic Pettman, who is also interviewed herein, recently applied that idea in the book *Metagestures* (punctum books, 2019), a mix of theory and fiction and an experiment in the spirit of that previous quotation.

ROY CHRISTOPHER: *As your hands hover over many heated pies, what would you say is the core of your work? If one were to call* *you just a historian, one would have to have a broad definition of the term!*

CARLA NAPPI: I've always been interested in the relationship between flesh and language, even as I've only recently become conscious of that interest. As an undergrad majoring in paleobiology, as a grad student writing about the history of natural history in early modern China, in the short fiction and poetry that I'm making more recently: on some level my work has always been exploring how we language creatures, including ourselves, and how languages fleshes us.

Words have always been material, living entities for me. When I've studied languages, it was never out of an interest in performing expertise in any of them, even as that was a necessary, professional side effect in some cases. Instead, I love the way new-to-me forms of language move my mind and body in unfamiliar ways, how they change my experience of the world and of the language (Italian-American, New York/New Jersey-area English) that is most fundamentally part of me.

I fell into history incidentally and in some ways accidentally. I had been obsessed with dinosaurs, and insects, and frogs, and other small creatures, from as early as I can remember. In high-school science geek camp, I read about the Burgess Shale fossils — super-wacky, pre-Cambrian invertebrates, many with body plans that don't exist anymore — and was completely hooked. In college I had every intention of being a paleontologist. At some point, with the help of some thoughtful mentors, I realized that the kinds of questions I was bringing to my work weren't really the sorts of questions that I could meaningfully explore in a lab space. Instead, they were getting in the way. And so I moved to a field where I was still asking questions about the transformations of forms of life in time but was working with an archive of documents instead of stones. And the stories that I was telling were increasingly born from an attention to the ways that language of all sorts shapes how we understand, and how people have understood, those transformations.

So, given all of that, I've never been interested in the sorts of things that historians are supposed to be interested in, such as explaining large-scale change over time, claiming to speak for people in the past, or really claiming to definitively know anything about anyone, past or present. I'm not interested in arguing with people about whose interpretation is correct or otherwise engaging in the agonistic environment of much of academic discourse, and I'm not so interested in trying to convince people to agree with me about... pretty much anything, really. Instead, the spirit of my work is to fully attend to the materials I work with, to bring my whole self to the project of seeing them and living with them, and to offer the results to others in the hope that they might be useful in some way. It's this spirit of whole-human-presence that informs how I think of my scholarly work as an art practice. You can imagine how polarizing this approach can be in academic spaces. There are real consequences, alternately nourishing and beautiful and painful and damaging. But it's who I am, and it's what I have to bring to the table.

RC: *One of the issues many scholars have with being interdisciplinary — or undisciplined — is tenure reviews and other such assessments tend to happen within rigid definitions of disciplines. Is that a concern for you? Or how do you negotiate that conflict?*

CN: Whew! This is a big one...

I struggle to answer this question without going negative. This has been part of the journey of the last year — getting out of the negative place. But let's start there so we can move out of it. When I first started doing this kind of work, it sucked. I mean, really, really sucked. I've spent so many breaks after so many talks blowing my nose and drying my eyes with conference hotel bathroom toilet paper. I've been yelled at — really, truly shouted at — by colleagues, that I had respected and admired, for "not speaking English," for presenting work that was strange and thus not being "kind" or "generous" enough to my audience, for stepping out of line ("Who does she think she is?"), for being "too performative" and thus not scholarly enough ("She apparently thinks she's being cute"). These are actual quotes. For being incoherent, for "making it sound like I know what I'm talking about," for being too much or not enough in all sorts of ways. I've been castigated for not performing in a way that demonstrates sufficient respect to "older and smarter" colleagues. I've been taken aside and condescended to, or publicly put in my place, more times than I can relate. I've been told explicitly that my work is not of value. I spent decades on the verge of leaving academia. Given that I have one finite, mortal life, why would I stay in a toxic environment where I constantly had to justify the value of my work and, by extension, my existence? The short answer for many years was that I needed the paycheck and that I loved my students. And on some level, I really thought it was possible to change things, to make the institution better. Now, I believe I'm not going to change academia. But just staying here and finding a way to exist and do my work and help other misfits do the same feels like enough. It feels like a lot. I try to be a small force for good by working in the interstices, by helping to make spaces in-between, by supporting the work of others who also find their fit with academia to be uneasy at best.

Peer review is still a problem. That experience is particularly difficult for me. I've spent so many years — publicly as a podcaster and behind the scenes in all sorts of ways — trying to help create a more generous space for engaging the work of colleagues, and that is so important to me, so when I feel like my work isn't being attended to in a spirit of generosity — and I mean *critical* generosity — it hurts badly. It's really damaging, and it has made me shy of publishing my work in many academic spaces. My feeling about this sort of reaction ("I just don't understand you") is to look harder; try again; challenge the way you attend to colleague's work; read more generously. I'm still working through that. Okay, so all of this is to say, yeah, it's a concern for me. And for my students. And for the other students and colleagues in this biz who have experienced, who are experiencing, anything similar. There are lots and lots of us. To do this kind of queer, a-disciplinary work in tenure-track academia, you have to do it on top of the normal, straight work. If you're lucky enough to find a department that likes having someone who does non-disciplinary work around, you still, most often, have to do that work as an addendum to the normal disciplinary stuff. You can be weird, but you still have to pass. And history is, relatively speaking, a *suuuuuuuuper* conservative academic space where peer review often shuts down experimental, non-disciplinary work unless it's done by an already established scholar who has developed a personal brand. I try to push against this in my capacity as a peer reviewer of others' work — in reference letters, tenure reviews, evaluations of job and grad student applications, and student work — to lift up colleagues who are working in unusual ways. I give talks about this. I write about it. I agitate in whatever ways that I can.

But this all centers the negative. And I mention it because there are lots and lots of us. Maybe someone out there is reading this, and they'll know they're not the only one. Maybe someone needs to know that today. And if my experience in academia were still largely this way, I would have left by now. It's only recently that I've committed to staying. And it's only recently that I've started to feel like I can make this job into what I need it to be in order to live and flourish in academia. From the very beginning, for me, academia was both the only career that felt right, that felt like it made sense as a professionplace to be fully myself, and a professionplace where I could never be fully myself. That conflict has always been there. And because of it, leaving academia is not obviously the right call. Neither is staying and trying to change myself into something I'm not. And so, the project is to try to stay and make it into what I need it to be in order for it not to feel toxic.

Much of my experience is largely positive these days, but that's really because I've made choices to stop putting myself in some situations and instead to inhabit and create other sorts of spaces. Since disciplinary communities were not welcoming in the ways that I needed them to be, I've formed other communities. In this business, as in life, finding your people is so important. The social and affective ties that bind us make our voices what they are, make them intelligible, or not. My ties and communities, for the most part right now, are not disciplinary ones.

And so, what I've decided to do in the midst of all of this is to really do it. Is to joyfully let go and embrace the challenge of making academia into what I — and others! — need it to be in order to flourish, and to do whatever comes next. Because I think I have relative security to do that — I think, I hope, I can pay my mortgage and my other bills and still do this — and honestly, it's a matter of life and death for some of us. And I have help, and I'm lucky to know some amazing people who are kindred spirits and who are similarly inclined. So, the prevailing spirit is *let's do this, let's at least try and see what comes.* One of my models in this spirit has been Lynda Sexson, one of my colleagues when I was working at Montana State University, who is a religious studies scholar, a fiction writer, a founder of the literary journal *Corona* that adopted me when I was a first-year faculty member at MSU, and just an amazing, brilliant human.

Academia as a professional space is still built on discipline. Because of that, perhaps to be a-disciplinary is also to be unprofessional. Which I'm fine with. The prizes, the accolades, the professional laurels: none of that stuff matters, beyond the basic animal level of it feeling good when people validate you, when you allow yourself to believe that the fact that they like you and your work means that you and your work must be of value. And I guess, in economic terms, that's what value is, isn't it? So, I guess if we're looking for a sense of value, we're looking economically. Okay, so if you're not deeply interested in that, then the question becomes, is it possible to exist here without that? What would a non-economic existence look like in academia?

From one important perspective — and this has been confirmed over and over again — what I do is not of value. So, rather than trying to scream its value into existence in a space where it's just necessarily and perhaps by definition going to fail, what about trying to find a practice where the value of the work is not what justifies its existence? Where its "value" is not the point nor the goal? So, in that case what is the point, what is the goal? What if there is none? What makes it worth doing? Well, "worth," as I just said, isn't the point here. So how do we even begin to talk about these questions? What would it be to live, academically, off the grid? I don't have answers. So maybe right now I'm trying to exist as an incoherent being. And maybe that's what historical pataphysics is, that is, the doomed-to-failure project of writing an incoherent history of incoherent beings. It necessarily has to fail on some level. But out of that failure grows... something? Something beautiful?

So that's what you do. You find your people, you support and nourish each other, you make spaces where you can flourish, and you cultivate relationships devoted to making stuff together with amazing people. You become a kind of gardener. I'm trying to be that kind of gardener. I'm not doing anything radical. All I'm doing is what I can do, the only thing I can do, which is to speak from where I am, to keep writing myself into existence until I can't anymore. I'm working with what I have to work with, as we all do, to grow things, to be with them as they come into existence and as they pass back out again, and to learn something from the process.

RC: *We talked before about how collaborative much of your work is. Many of us struggle with working well with others. I'm sure it varies, but how do you approach these projects?*

CN: Collaboration is so important to me. Most of my work now is explicitly collaborative, and that's not the norm in my fields. I've done my share of collaboration out of a sense that we ought to work together because our areas of expertise overlapped in some way. Given my experience with that sort of collaboration, it's not something that I do anymore.

These days, for me, collaboration always starts with a personal connection, a sense that I have some sort of energy with another person and we want to make something together. The specifics of what we make come later. And that takes care of the working-well-with-others problem, which, believe me, I share! The relationship comes first, and the object we make grows out

27

of that. The people I'm working with now are all people that I expect to be working with for the rest of my life in different ways. And because I'm devoted to the collaborative relationships that I currently have, and I really want to honor those relationships by feeding them with the time and attention they need, I hesitate to take on a new collaboration unless I really feel like it's something we both want to commit to, something that will feel energizing rather than draining, something that we both look forward to working on instead of feeling obligated to turn to.

Different collaborations take different forms. Sometimes we'll travel together to do research. Sometimes we have regular Skypewine conversations that incorporate our work together and from which some of that work grows. In all cases, there's some anchor keeping us grounded, whether it's a text we're reading together or a set of objects we're attending to together or some common experience that we can come back to in order to give our conversation form.

Oddly, my collaborations now include work with nonhuman partners. I bought a house in Pittsburgh last year, and as a way to get to know the house, which truly is a living organism and is very much my domestic partner, I've been writing stories with it. They've turned into an ongoing project that's a kind of hybrid cookbook, lifestyle guide, and work of short kooky fictions.

And sometimes the collaborations make forms of life — inventing unusual ways of being and working together and supporting and caring for each other, ways of being kin — in the process of creating written objects together, and when that happens it's such a joy. In a real way, the writing becomes a precipitate of that greater form of collaboration and co-making. And I think you can see that in the work.

RC: *In 2013 you did a colloquium at University of California, Berkeley about DJs, sampling, and history. Can you tell me about this talk? Do you have any plans to revisit the idea?*

CN: For years, I've been interested in the meaning that comes from putting things next to each other. I've been writing a lot about hashtags and constellations and sedimentation.

Several years ago, I took a digital DJing course and my first baby steps in learning the craft. I was immediately struck by how similar the art of a DJ was, at least as I was learning and experiencing it, to that of a historian. We amass archives, we tell stories that have a kind of narrative arc, we work with time as a material. Sampling is a kind of quotation. Distortion and other effects are ways of reading a musical text. There are just so many resonances, and I felt that thinking about these crafts together could be a way of informing and inspiring both of them.

Then I started listening to Girl Talk. A lot. And I kept coming back to the question, what would it be to do this for the materials I work with?

I started in the classroom, working with digital sampling tech and a drum pad to compose with Sappho's fragments in a lecture that I do about her work. That lecture also involves transforming the room into a drum pad.

And then this past year I got a new Traktor controller and pulled out my old training and dusted it off and started working with the tech to really experiment with what it could be to remix documents. After many, many hours and a notebook in which I've been recording a kind of autoethnography of the process, what that has turned into is a practice not of translating the documents themselves into sound files and working with them that way but instead of translating the forms of attention I bring to sound when I'm working with Traktor to my eighteenth-century Manchu documents. I'm just at the beginning, but it has been completely rad. I did a kind of performance-talk based on this material at the Gray Center at University of Chicago last fall, and I'm working up a textual piece for them that extends the project into a space that considers the relationship between DJing, history, and Tarot. It's wild. There's much more to come. It might turn into a book. It needs to grow at its own pace, and I'll see.

RC: *Your* Metagestures *book with Dominic Pettman, who is also interviewed in this volume, just came out. What's that all about?*

CN: Oh, I love this book so much. Thank you for asking.

Dominic and I met at an event that was supposed to be a living bestiary. He did this amazing talk as the Horse Guy, and I did my first-ever public reading of a work of my short fiction as the Phoenix Girl. We were arranged in the schedule according to the size of the creature we were embodying, and no one could figure out where to put the phoenix. And we knew pretty much immediately that we wanted to work together somehow. So I interviewed him for a book-interview podcast, and we started reading stuff together, and eventually we did a performance that smooshed together books we were each writing and that were each inspired by Italo Calvino's *Invisible Cities,* and that performance was so inspiring for the both of us that we decided to try to write something together. We were both thinking of that writing as a kind of conversation, and this would be a way to talk and think together. So then we needed to find some sort of an anchor for that conversation, something we could each write from. At some point he suggested Vilém Flusser's book *Gestures* as an anchor, and, once we started it, we realized it was perfect.

From the beginning, then, the project that became *Metagestures* was very much an experiment in reading together as much as writing together. We tried all sorts of methods of co-reading. Sometimes we would just set a chapter of Flusser's book and agree to exchange our responses to the chapter by a particular deadline. Sometimes we would open a chat window and read the same pages at the same time, making notes for each other as we read and simultaneously having a conversation about them, which is super fun and a method we still use. For one pair of stories, we came up with a common set of narrative elements — the characters, the arc of the story, particular details — and each wrote our own version of the same story that incorporated those elements. (That was probably my favorite process. We'll do that again.) The funny thing was that we never intentionally set out to write a book of fictions. We just both started writing them as a way to be in conversation with Flusser's work and with each other. And we wanted to find a way to make space in academia for the kind of joyful, non-disciplinary, experimental engagement with the work of other scholars. Working with academic theory doesn't have to look like writing academic theory. Fiction can be itself and can also be a thoughtful product of very rigorous research. That's what this book is.

So, the book itself is a product of that extended experiment in reading and writing together. It collects thirty-two short stories, sixteen pairs that sequentially move the reader through the gestures that make up the chapters of Flusser's book: the gesture of listening, of painting, of turning a mask around, of shaving, and on and on. We wanted it to read both as a book of short fictions that demanded zero knowledge of or interest in Flusser, and also as a kind of response to Flusser's work on gesture for readers who were interested in that aspect of the project. Each of us, in our respective set of stories, worked with and emphasized aspects of Flusser's work that we found most inspiring at the time. So, in my stories you'll see the importance of self-recognition and its connection to enchantment and divinity come up a bunch of times.

We've been working together on a new project that we're calling *The Poetics of Space Opera,* reading Gaston Bachelard, and more Flusser, together, and feeling our way towards a shape of writing that makes sense. It's a great joy, and we're at the very beginning. Stay tuned!

RC: *What's coming up next for you?*

CN: Oh, so much.

I'm working with Dianna Frid, a brilliant artist based in Chicago, on a project called "Wormholes," where we travel to rare book collections that contain insect-damaged materials and we read with the worms, with the traces of the creatures that have come before us. We're working on the first fruits of a recent trip to the Burgoa Library in Oaxaca.

Carrie Jenkins, a brilliant writer and philosopher based in Vancouver, and I are putting the finishing touches on a book of poetry inspired and talking back to Plato's *Symposium,* currently titled *Uninvited: Talking Back to Plato,* and we expect it to come out in 2020. We've also been working together on a website called *The Invisible College* on which we share work-in-progress of all sorts and post wine-soaked conversations about assorted academia-and-life-related things, and we're hatching plans for further collaborative shenanigans.

Speaking of further shenanigans, there is much more to come with Dominic Pettman, another brilliant human. Among other things, we've been working to make a space for work that doesn't comfortably fit in the normal academic spaces with the free electronic pamphlet press *Flugschriften,* and we're excited about where that's going.

With Judy Farquhar, a brilliant anthropologist and human, I've been co-shepherding a collective of anthropologists, artists, healers of various sorts, historians, and other makers and scholars in a long-running project called Translating Vitalities. We'll be continuing to gather around themes broadly related to translating forms of life, and up next is a series of gatherings in North Carolina and Berlin that orient toward reading as a creative practice of attention.

I'll also be trying to find homes for some misfit booktoys that I love to pieces. I've been working for many years on a hybrid fiction/history book about translation in early-modern China. And I have a strange collection of very short stories about historians of elemental substance, all named Elizabeth, that I've been writing and performing for a couple of years, and that also wants a home.

I'm trying to write with my insomnia, and just began a new project that explores what history that inhabits an insomniac temporality might look like.

And I'm on the cusp of launching The Laboratory for Historical Pataphysics at the University of Pittsburgh, which will be all kinds of wacky and awesome.

2

KRISTEN GALLERNEAUX
Unattended Consequences

Interview and illustration by Roy Christopher
June 24, 2019

Whether you believe in ghosts or not, you are haunted. Your browser crashes under the weight of open tabs. Your phone buzzes with unanswered calls. You worry over unpaid bills. There are others hiding in your devices, spirits swirling in their circuitry.

In another time, Kristen Gallerneaux would've been considered a sorcerer, a witch, a medium. She coaxes the ghosts from black boxes of all kinds. In our time, Gallerneaux is an artist, a writer, a researcher, and the Curator of Communication and Information Technology at The Henry Ford Museum in Detroit. She also holds a PhD in Art Practice & Media History from University of California, San Diego, an MA in Folklore from the University of Oregon, and an MFA in Art from Wayne State University. Her book, *High Static, Dead Lines* (Strange Attractor/MIT Press, 2018) is a travel journal of her explorations of technologies past, a memoir of hidden hauntings.

ROY CHRISTOPHER: *From the outside, you seem to have a very unique position between curator, artist, and author. How does it look from the inside?*

KRISTEN GALLERNEAUX: It can get a little complicated balancing the time commitments, ethics, and future-casting of these roles. My art practice too can be further fractured into many segments, whether I'm working on sound or image production. I tend to work in sprints — a few weeks of solid writing or field recording and music production, a few months of pairing those results with manipulated video footage — then figuring out how to turn everything into an intriguing shareable format, whether a live multimedia presentation or a publishable context. And my curatorial gig is a full-time position too, so I'm in the office plotting and planning for, writing about, researching, interpreting, and acquiring historic technology and communications objects by day. I find a lot of inspiration for my art and writing practices in my curatorial work, so there's a lot energy exchange between the borders of those roles. There's certainly a slight division in how I write about objects as a public historian versus my more literary, speculative modes required by some of my personal research topics.

A lot of people who become professional curators go full sonic force and give up their personal art practices, or maybe that curatorial impulse turned out to be the strongest urge all along. When I landed a full-time curatorial role, I was so consumed and excited about learning the ropes that I might have considered retiring from art making in the first year or so, but I take it all back now! There is that impulse when you find a job you love, to just give your entire life over. But following the models of people like Sister Corita Kent — "The only rule is work. If you work it will lead to something" — or the play-experimentation of Charles and Ray Eames, I've settled into something more balanced, more humane, that allows for both. Ultimately, I am a bit of a homebody, carving out creative time over nights and weekends.

I do tend to say yes to a lot of things. I generally just thrive on taking on a challenge and whatever I can learn from it even if its slightly outside of my comfort range. There have been times where I get myself in too deep and deadlines can pile up to the point where it can feel like everything is going to fall apart.

I don't like to be defined by it, but, whether I like to admit it or not, my personal and professional practices lives are complicated at times by a few long-term, physical health issues that impact my energy levels and sleep cycles. I have a really strict structure I stick to in order to stave off symptoms. For instance, despite my love of live music, I'm not exactly capable of staying out until 3 a.m. to catch an event or rave until sunrise. And there are still those inexplicable times when, despite my best efforts, I'll suddenly be slammed with insomnia and not able to sleep more than three or four hours a night for several months. These forced slowdowns are annoying as hell, but I try to push through so that I'm not dwelling on "why do I feel this way, how are all of these symptoms connected, and why can't five different doctors figure this out?"

I guess I embrace the potential for chaos a little bit, too. I enjoy a lot of music and art that feels like it's barely holding itself together. There are examples that are so elemental — like Rabit's chopped & screwed track "Still Tipping" or those that utilize such an excess of space, like Dale Cornish's *Cut Sleeve* EP — that I can't help but laugh and think, "how is that even allowed?" But oh man, it makes me so happy! Likewise, I love things that are so dense or charged that they seem illegible or mysteriously unknowable, like Dario Robleto's early work, Rammellzee's world-making mythologies and Gothic Futurism,[1] and the visual density of core memory stacks. There's the peak and crumble of amplified, slowed, or intense sonic palettes of The Bug, Emptyset, and that one time I saw a bass battle in Miami with Dave Tompkins. And there are those giddy whirls of emotion that come from being confronted by visually or experientially dense typologies out in the wild.

I encounter this a lot in museum storage spaces, but it can happen in random ways too, like going to it's-so-early-it's-still-dark-out swap meets whenever I visit my friend Steve in Cali-

---

1 See Chuck Galli's interview with Rammellzee in this volume.

fornia. One time we went to this place called Yoshi's Warehouse in an old Nabisco Factory in Fresno. It was filled with literal heaps and towering, crash-over-on-you stacks of junk. Mountains of jumbled up clothes hangers. I found a solo white go-go boot sitting on top of a red IBM Selectric typewriter in there, and that's an image I can't scrub from my brain, ever. One time I toured Detroit's then-abandoned Packard Plant with the artist Scott Hocking, and the floor of one room was covered in melted-together, interior car-door panels. It was like a terrifying bouncy castle with random shards of wood and crumbling plastic. Outside, we could hear a team of scrappers quite literally disassembling the building's beam construction with acetylene torches. Poignant stuff I find compelling; not sure if anyone else does though.

RC: *High Static, Dead Lines is a blend of genres (e.g., memoir, media archaeology, criticism, history, etc.). Was this mix by design, or did it just come out that way?*

KG: I think it's only fair to credit Brian Cross, a.k.a. B+, here, who read the early manuscript of what eventually became *High Static* while he was my PhD advisor. He was one of the first people to state out loud that the project was "like a mixtape." It was always intentional, even unavoidable, given my interdisciplinary background, that this is how the book was meant to take shape. I was pretty nervous in the lead-up to its publication. I wasn't sure if it would end up getting panned for having such a blatant mixture of literary works colliding with media history essays. But I like to think there are ample through-lines, themes, and rhythms that tie it together, small and large, that allow you to skip around but that are also "object lesson"-type essays that go in depth on content.

I've always had a somewhat contentious relationship with traditional academia, but I found hope in academic programs that allowed space for interdisciplinary exploration at "high" and "low" levels of culture if you believe in that kind of division.

I was incredibly lucky to find a publisher at Strange Attractor/MIT Press that allowed me all the running room I could ever hope for, and they never doubted the format. I think ultimately, I wanted to replicate the feeling of being invited to share in the discovery of an intriguing research "rabbit hole," the high weirdness of hidden histories, or maybe even that hard-to-pin-down feeling you get when people start sharing family ghost stories at a social gathering, totally unprompted. Depending where you open the book, these are the experiences I wanted to invoke.

There was an important cumulative effect on my work, encountering the copasetic work of others that helped opened the doors of permission to make a book like High Static. Discovering ficto-criticism through Lesley Stern, as well as Steven O'Connor's looping, micro-macro writing about objects, Wayne Koestenbaum's visual fictions in his "Legend" column of Cabinet magazine, Allen C. Shelton's *Dreamworlds of Alabama*'s refrigerators as hauntological time-machines, Mark Alice Durant's essay in the *Blur of the Otherworldly* exhibition catalog, *Stop Smiling* magazine, and Mark Fisher's psychic imprints of landscape and sound media. But really, I think the book that blew the doors completely off for me was Dave Tompkins's *How to Wreck a Nice Beach*—that poetic blend of technology, cultural and sonic history, personal narrative, heavy use of illustration and photos—and it continues to blow my mind a decade later. Over the years, Dave has become a great friend, mentor, and was one of the first people to encourage me to write a book.

So yeah, I guess *High Static* is a culmination and a bit of a homage to those experiences, as well as a bit of an exorcism of familial folklore and the more gothic aspects of "growing up weird" in a small town.

RC: *The black-boxing of our technologies, in the Latourian sense, has always intrigued and frustrated me in equal measure. I've been thinking through it via music-playback devices: we used to share our cassette- and CD-cases. That is, we could determine what each other was listening to by looking at our portable stash. It was a way to get to know someone. Since the .mp3 became the portable medium, I've seen less of this as those choices are black-boxed into the device. Has this been your experience?*

KG: Yeah, definitely! I love the idea of mystery of the seemingly unknowable thing that wants to swallow up its own tail. It implies a sense of liveliness to things that are supposed to be static. I often joke that I am a curator who deals with brown, black, and silver boxes of various shades and shapes. It's a joke, but also totally true when you think of wood-cased radios evolving into the rectangular convergence glitz of smartphones. There's also that macro-micro fascination embedded in there — the density of information building up through tubes, wires, and silicon chips, you know? So, there's the actual media player aspect to consider in addition to the formats they play. Peeling back another level, there is also the materiality of the encoded information that exists on magnetic tape, optical discs, or as pure bits and bytes. I'd have to defer to people like Jonathan Sterne, Patrick Feaster, or Paul Dourish here, who have all written incredible studies on the history of sound formats.

It's hard to talk about this black boxing of media and not seem nostalgic, like one of those "in the good ol' days, we had 78s and 8-bit graphics" kind of people. But as a kid of the 1980s and '90s, I know I'm not alone in having an affection for the physical artifact and the emotional connection of exchanging a mix on cassette or CD, or even writing out a track list by hand. Some of the mixtape exchanges I had as a teenager helped to define who I am today. I wasn't a wealthy kid, and neither were my friends, so there was a shared library of tapes and CDs that we passed around and copied from one another. It's important, however, to point out that these exchanges were only established thanks to friendships formed over Bulletin Board Systems that I accessed on my Amiga 500 in the '90s. So, for me at least, there was this funny juxtaposition of emergent digital and analog tech existing in a confused feedback loop in a tiny rural town in Canada.

The sharing culture of teenagers has obviously morphed drastically since the days of the www. There is a loss of time spent hunting for that elusive cultural artifact, whatever it may be. Today you can make your own discoveries in relative isolation, no longer needing to meet the right network of people who share your music tastes, knowing the "right" magazines to read or record stores to shop at. Prior to the web, the assumption was that your town was large or cultured enough to even have these resources, and mine certainly wasn't, so thank god for those monochrome message boards! I suppose this is all describing its own kind of cultural black box, right?

The breadth of cultural access and the immediate satisfaction possible, that is, to pull up some trace of the thing you want to hear or discover on the web, has completely rewired the brains of young people, for better and for worse. Despite a lack of physical formats, we can't claim that sharing and exchange culture has entirely vanished — perhaps just truncated through one-off media exchanges. Same outcome, different formats?

Between my husband's and my media collections, our house is overflowing with our mutual autobiographies, collected in many different physical formats, thousands of books and records, hundreds of tapes, and thousands of CDs. And then there everything on the computer, which is mostly out-of-sight-out-of-mind for me. Sometimes we have a digital duplicate a thing that also exists in physical form, there is the file that only ever existed digitally, the shared Dropboxes, and streaming platforms. It all gets to be a bit much, but not enough to make me want to "Marie Kondo" my media collection.

RC: *Have you seen it in other media?*

KG: It definitely applies to other media. Some of my earliest memories were of the video-game arcade that my family ran in the 1980s. Classic retro-bait. Digging around in the guts of broken *Space Invaders* machines in the game graveyard in the back of the arcade. Standing on an overturned bucket to watch my brothers play *Galaga* or whatever, that communal trade-off effect of teenagers peering over one another's shoulders to absorb in the experience in the present moment. Or something as simple as sneaking a glance of people's book covers during a bus commute, rather than the backsides of Kindles or smartphones. With analog media, it can seem easiest to say there is an opportunity to stumble upon shared experiences and random connection through the blurring of public/private consumption of culture. A statement that might make me sound like a bit of a Luddite, which I'm absolutely not.

RC: *With streaming the dominant playback mode these days, there's such an "on-demand" sense of media and media artifacts. In light of the recent MySpace server-migration debacle,[2] what happens to culture when there's nothing there to "demand"?*

KG: Not sure how to fully answer this without casting too much hope on *The Wayback Machine* or *The Internet Archive*. The aforementioned BBS spaces that I dwelled in in the '90s have all but vaporized too. Movie rental stores are basically gone except for a few niche examples, which makes it impossible to browse and discover things accidentally, a process that I require in life. With on-demand streaming, the sparkle has worn off for me lately, especially when it comes to film. What is being offered up feels so hollow, when you see through the lines, you know it is only an illusion of a world of choice. There are profoundly huge and concerning swaths of film history that are being lost to the algorithm and streaming distribution battles. There are the titles that will never be recommended, as your searches are filtered by algorithms. Why does my Amazon Fire Stick refuse to recognize a voice search for Dario Argento? It's really not that obscure a name these days.

RC: *Is all media haunted? I mean, connotations aside, is there a medium that is spirit-proof?*

---

2 See Cory Doctorow, "Facebook is Next," *bOING bOING*, March 17, 2019, https://boingboing.net/2019/03/17/facebook-is-next.html.

KG: I'd like to think that any kind of media or object that has the potential for degradation also carries the possibility of feeling "haunted." I guess another question is, how far do we allow the boundaries to expand when deciding what media is? Is dirt media? Are those gross human hair wreaths from the nineteenth century media? I kind of think they are. I have a collection of soil samples from purportedly haunted locations. So does that mean dirt could be haunted? Are the "cursed objects" that weirdos and hucksters sell on eBay haunted media?

It's really about the 1+1=3 approach, where a straightforward substrate collides with human presence and is interpreted as behaving in a way that is perceived as unexpected or "wrong." An imprinted or affectual presence results in a third, unexpected layer of experience that can feel charged.

Using sound as evidence of the afterlife has been written about extensively, from séance rooms to EVP evidence, so I won't repeat that here. But just like photography and film, the evolution of any kind of media entering paranormal cultural studies or investigation expands as technology expands. It was only a matter of time before someone took a relatively mundane tool, like, say Google Street View, and layered their own interpretation of glitches as being supernaturally derived. Black smears that might be wraiths or just garbage bags in a ditch. Cloud formations interpreted as alien or angelic. People with smeared out faces straight out of a J-Horror movie.

My husband and I used to live in a house from the 1860s in Detroit. We heard that it had been squatted in the 1970s and '80s, and it's a safe assumption to make that some nefarious events occurred there over the years. A few times a year, there would be these strange cycles where the vibe of the place would feel "off," let's say. Suddenly our pets would be chasing unseen things into corners. My husband was once standing in the kitchen and a piece of plaster from above the cupboard flew across the room and hit him in the head. The lightbulbs would start blowing out at a rapid rate. We know from the very long history of supernatural stories that architecture has the potential to act as haunted media too, along with all of the objects and systems within, from exploding lightbulbs to the creaks and groans of the building itself.

RC: *What's coming up for you?*

KG: I've been traveling over the last two years in the US and Europe presenting different iterations and creative productions that are based on material that appears in *High Static*. All the while, I've been mulling over the next project, which is loosely going to focus on the cultural history of fragments, fissures, and fractures. As I was writing *High Static,* this became a kind of orphan topic that didn't make a ton of sense in that book but was better saved for another project. In June 2019, I was selected as one of the Kresge Detroit Artist Fellows. As I write this, the announcement is about to go live in a few days, and I'm looking forward to the financial support, time, and community-building associated with that award. I'll have the resources to travel to museums, private collections, and historic sites, and I'm expecting to encounter a lot of unexpected things along the way. I've been slowly working on an LP over the last few years too, which is built off of sonifying the archive of "haunted" soil samples that I mentioned earlier and from field recordings that were made in the types of landscapes that Mark Fisher would have classified as "eerie."

Professionally, I'm continuing to build up the technology collections for the museum, mostly focusing on bolstering up the post-WWII histories in computing, graphic communications, and so on. I just finished co-curating an exhibit with a colleague called *Break, Repair, Repeat: Spontaneous and Improvised Design,* which led myself and another curator to root through our storage areas to find artifacts with interesting and purposeful alterations. Some favorite moments in the exhibit include an eighteenth-century teapot with a repaired silver spout displayed near a circuit-bent Speak & Spell that was turned into a musical instrument. Or a repaired weathervane next to an early assistive speech/vision technology known as a Votrax Speak & Spell. It's all about using the messiness of ingenuity to provide solutions to human-object and design problems. And a little bit of the "right amount of wrong."

3

DOMINIC PETTMAN
Human Matters

Interview by Roy Christopher
Illustration by Josh Row
April 23, 2018

I first came across Dominic Pettman's work through his 2011 book, *Human Error: Species-Being and Media Machines* (University of Minnesota Press), which deftly connected so many things I am interested in. Not long after, he wrote a cultural history of my favorite animal, *Look at the Bunny: Totem, Taboo, Technology* (Zero Books, 2013). He had written several before, and he's written several since. He is a professor at Eugene Lang College and also teaches in the Liberal Studies Program at the New School for Social Research. Pettman is currently both one of my favorite theorists and one of my favorite writers.

I can't introduce him without pointing you to his *In Divisible Cities: A Phanto-Cartographical Missive* (Dead Letter Office/punctum books, 2013). It's a poetic, aphoristic urban excursion. You can download or buy it directly from punctum books or lose yourself in Alli Crandell's interactive web version at https://indivisiblecities.punctumbooks.com/.

ROY CHRISTOPHER: *What would you say is your area of work?*

DOMINIC PETTMAN: My official title is Professor of Culture & Media, so I guess that gives an accurate idea of the scope of my beat. In other words, pretty much anything is fair game! My university education in Australia was quite eclectic and promiscuous, and we were not encouraged to squat on a sub-sub-field as many are here in the States. So, I never learned to get the laser vision that some of my colleagues have. When I arrived in the US in 2004, where people described my writing as "brave," it took me a while to figure out that this was code for "crazy and reckless." Nevertheless, it's too late for me to hyper-specialize now.

I do, however, have enduring themes that I'm interested in, and my work pays particular attention to questions concerning the species-being of "the human," especially in relation to the technical aspects of various libidinal economies and ecologies. For the past twenty years, my research has focused on neglected connections between philosophical ideas, psychological states, social anxieties, and cultural artifacts, with a particular focus on the media used to create and navigate these phenomena. While the objects of my research may seem quite different from project to project, they are all case studies relating to the three main questions animating my work: 1) How do humans use media/technology to symbolize their complex experience of time? 2) How do humans use media/technology to communicate their conflicted experience of intersubjectivity? And 3) how do humans use media/technology to perpetuate, or complicate, their ambivalent relationships to other forms of intelligence, such as animals or machines?

In one recent book, *Infinite Distraction: Paying Attention to Social Media* (Polity, 2016), I demonstrate the ways in which online sharing platforms "hypermodulate" our attention in order to more effectively control our behavior, via different digital rhythms and time signatures. In another recent title, *Sonic Intimacy: Voice, Species, Technics* (Stanford University Press, 2017), I ask why it is that humans have historically been considered the only being blessed with voice. I proceed from there to explore the notion that animals and machines may in fact have their own modes of "speech" and may thus be trying to tell us something that we are currently incapable of hearing. A companion title, *Creaturely Love: How Desire Makes Us More and Less Than Human* (University of Minnesota Press, 2017), details some of the ways that desire makes us both more, and less, than human by looking closely at some canonical literary, philosophical, and aesthetic uses of animalistic themes, within the lovers' discourse.

RC: *You are quite prolific, having finished as many books as I've started in the same amount of time, as well as posting regularly online. Do you have an elaborate writing scheme and schedule? Are there really two of you?*

DP: I'm somewhat abashed to say that I don't. I'm not one of these people that write a little bit a day, and then, by the end of the year, I find I have 100k words ready to go. Rather, I tinker a little bit with notes as I circle the project, and, then, when the moment feels right, I pounce and work like crazy until it's finished. I definitely need a clear block of time in order to bring a manuscript together, whether this be a summer break or a sabbatical. Also, what you might notice is that my books are getting shorter and shorter. One day I aspire to be Giorgio Agamben and have even a haiku published as a book in a 5,000-point font. But I can work quickly. *Infinite Distraction,* for instance, was written during a four-week winter break. Of course, it sold more copies and got more attention than the book I spent several years on! There's a lesson there perhaps.

But usually when people ask what the secret is, I tell them don't have kids. Then again, my colleague, McKenzie Wark is a very committed parent, and she is even more prolific than I am. Maybe it's an Australian thing.

Seriously though, I do think that many academics or theorists, especially those traumatized by grad school, tend to be wary of sharing anything with the world until it is so polished as to be mortified. There is also a fear that if you haven't read every single text even vaguely pertaining to your subject then you have no right to enter the conversation. But I prefer to see each book as a moment, or specific contribution, not the very last word on an issue. And this frees me up to address any gaps or unconsidered angles in a subsequent work.

RC: *Since you write about so many different topics, I am curious as to what is coming up next.*

DP: My current research, speaking generally, seeks more explicitly to "reanimalize the human" in order to more consciously track the ways in which our historical sense of human purpose ("species-being") is being challenged by and responding to new ethological discoveries, and a rather urgent new sense of ecological entanglement, not to mention mutual precarity.

I am in the midst of two manuscripts that emerge from this research. The first outlines a general "libidinal ecology," beginning with the provocative notion, borrowed from Bernard Stiegler, that we are running out of libido in the same way that we are running out of natural resources, like fresh water or oil. It begins by asking: "what is the carbon footprint of your libido?" — a quantitative conceit to clear the way for qualitative questions around desire, mobility, and media. Part of this project scans the archive of philosophical commentaries on human intimacy in search of seeds which never took root, which have the potential to free us from the dangers of "peak libido" and the associated impasses or afflictions of contemporary private life. Plato's *Symposium,* for instance, offers an array of definitions of human passions, but only Aristophanes's figure of the sutured "Hermaphrodite," fusing the self back together with its other half, has come to dominate the romantic imagination. What if we follow more nuanced accounts of what it means to be an in-dividual among other individuals, none of whom, perhaps, are as in-dividual as they may like to think?

The second project is more creative in spirit: an engagement with Vilém Flusser's theory of mediated gestures. This collaborative endeavor, with historian Carla Nappi featured in this collection, experiments with the written and performative forms through which scholars might engage and communicate media theory. This has yielded a complete manuscript, *Meta-Gestures,* which gathers together short stories written in tandem, responding to Flusser's original gestures, such as "the gesture of photographing," "the gesture of making," and "the gesture of planting." Can only humans make authentic gestures? Or can this specific type of semiosis — less than an action but more than an intention — be something performed also by animals and machines? Together, Carla and I intend to make an audit of contemporary gestures made in response to intensifying digital imperatives, while also creating a blueprint of alternative gestures which, at least potentially, embody the kind of "freedom" that Flusser himself felt must follow the rather dismal options provided by the program industries.

Ultimately, this research is conducted in the service of recognizing and fostering not only new forms of intimacy and understanding between radically different types of being but new conceptions of what it means to be human in a (productively!) dehumanized world.

4

RITA RALEY
Tactical Humanities

Interview by Roy Christopher
Illustration by Laura Persat
October 16, 2017

A professor in English with appointments in Film and Media Studies, Comparative Literature, and Global Studies at the University of California, Santa Barbara, Rita Raley studies all sorts of things that culminate in interesting intersections. She centers her study of tactical media, a designation Geert Lovink called a "deliberately slippery term," on disturbance. Her book on the subject, *Tactical Media* (University of Minnesota Press, 2009), illustrates not only the ways in which media participate in events but also her own nuanced thinking about and through that participation. She and her colleagues have also been busy dissecting Mark Z. Danielewski's twenty-seven-volume novel-in-progress, (five of which are currently available), *The Familiar*, of which Matthew Kirschenbaum calls Raley, "perhaps his best current reader."

ROY CHRISTOPHER: *What would you say is your area of work?*

RITA RALEY: Quite broadly, I would say: new media, aesthetics and politics, contemporary literature, and what we might call the machinic and geopolitical dimensions of language in the present, by which I mean investigations of the transformations that have occurred in our reading and writing practices in tandem with the development and widespread adoption of computational platforms for everyday communicative use. Concretely, this last has led me to think about machine reading, writing, and translation, alongside of electronic literature, code poetics, global English, and networked forms of expression from spam to picture languages. At the moment I am grouping these forms and practices together under the rubric of the post-alphabetic.

RC: *I haven't read Danielewski since* House of Leaves. *How would you convince fans of that book to invest in the lengthy journey that he has only just begun with* The Familiar?

RR: Life is short, our attention spans are shorter, and the perfect antidote to the sense that the world is slipping from our grasp is deep immersion in a serial narrative that prods us to be self-conscious about historical and planetary time on the one hand and our lived experience in the moment on the other. It rewards deep reading, as Danielewski's texts always do, and there are ample pleasures to be found in the decoding of the text's many puzzles and in the following of its lines of reference and inquiry out to other texts and bodies of knowledge, from AI to physics. But its pleasures are not only cerebral. It is at core — I want to say underneath its shimmering surface, which has been meticulously designed and crafted from cover to cover, but what I really mean is at its heart — a fantastic story. What might seem in volume 1 to be a set of stories, told in different genres, voices, and fonts, starts to converge over the course of the first season, volumes 1 through 5, and it's clear that everything is moving toward a spectacular convergence that is either going to be apocalyptically destructive or truly regenerative and probably a bit of both. There are many things to say, and many things have been said, about what Danielewski does with and for codex as a medium and all of that pertains to *The Familiar* as well. What differentiates the project from *House of Leaves* and *Only Revolutions* — and I say this with the awareness that they are situated in a shared or parallel diegetic world — is the scale. That its planned run is twenty-seven volumes makes this seem obvious perhaps, but there is something different in the orientation. *House of Leaves* and *Only Revolutions* seem to me to turn in on themselves, opening up and mining abyssal structures or systems by which they then seem to be absorbed. *The Familiar* rather gestures out and beyond. Its span is Alpha to Omega, and it wants not to plunge us into the trapdoor beneath our feet but to show us the stars.

RC: *Is there a such thing anymore as Humanities that are not Digital?*

RR: No.

But to answer that more seriously, I would say all knowledge work in the twenty-first-century university has been transformed — how could it not be? — but computational media are just part of the story. Paradigmatic changes in scholarly methods and practices are evident across the disciplines, and they are all in part attributable to the development of new tools, platforms, and techniques, but understanding the significance of all of this requires some consideration of the evolution of the idea of the university: what is its function and purpose, now; what are its products; what constituencies does it serve; why should institutional culture be defined by vision statements, agenda setting, and entrepreneurial activity? So, indeed, there has been what is often termed a "turn" to quantification, visualization, and making as both the means and end of knowledge production, but this shift is by no means particular to the humanities alone.

To be even more serious, I think that at least some humanities scholars should continue to think about, and with, that which is not-digital, not in the sense of what has been left behind but rather in the sense of what cannot be captured. The accelerations that we seem collectively to sense, in AI research, climate change, and tribal realignments, are in fact real, and we need to put our minds to reimagining a world that is not only inhabitable but worth preserving. How can, and should, we live in common, with each other and with nonhuman things? For these questions the humanities need not only engineering but also the environmental and social sciences.

RC: *I want to go back to your work on tactical media. How broadly do you define the concept?*

RR: I remain agnostic about what is or what is not "properly" tactical media. If it seems like a nail, use the hammer. If it works, if it gets the job done, whatever the job, great. The only way to guard against the inertia, apathy, and depression that often results from defeat is to act, but at some level we all have to decide for ourselves what constitutes a meaningful action. My own view is that now, in 2017, sharing ideas about the future and a common purpose are more important than sharing a definition.

5

JODI DEAN
Of Crowds and Collectives

Interview by Alfie Bown
Illustration by Eleanor Purcell
April 10, 2016

In this crisis for capitalism, Jodi Dean's new book, *Crowds and Party* (Verso Books, 2018), asks arguably the most important question of all: how do we turn our dissatisfaction with the situation and our willingness to take to the streets into organized political action that might lead to change? Her book, unlike many other "radicals" today, is interested in the concrete and practical ways in which dissatisfaction and protest can turn into organization and opposition. How does a crowd become a party, and what does that mean? Jodi Dean's book rejects those who invest positively in the individual or the multiple per se and instead asks for a new and more subversive collective subject of politics. From real crowds like the Occupy Movement to the theoretical conceptions of crowds and mobs, Dean's book interrogates the role of the crowd and the party in an attempt to provide a way forward politically.

ALFIE BOWN: *Let's start with crowds. Your book is interested in the role of the crowd historically and today, and when you discuss crowds, you make a distinction between the mob and the* *people. Do the people always have to become the mob, you ask? Could you say something about the difference between the two, and about how his distinction between the mob and the people is determined politically?*

JODI DEAN: You hit on the answer in your question: the distinction between the mob and the people is determined politically.

What I have in mind is the struggle over the interpretation of a crowd event. Generally speaking, mob has a negative, potentially fascistic, connotation, for example, "angry" mob or "lynch" mob. "Crowd" is more ambiguous. It gets interesting when people fight over the description of a particular crowd: is this a crowd, with some potential connection to the people struggling for freedom and equality, some connotation of the masses who are right to assemble and demand, or is it just a violent mob?

The fight over the description of the crowd is opened up by the crowd itself. A crowd amasses. Now, what does this mean? This depends on the perspective from which the crowd is viewed. From say, a conservative perspective, a perspective that fears the people, that worries about the disruptive capacity of the many, a crowd might look like a mob. From a communist perspective, this same crowd might look like the revolutionary people bringing a new Commune into being.

I am not saying that the crowd is always a crowd, never a mob, and that any assessment of the crowd as a mob is necessarily conservative. What I'm saying is that the disruption of the intrusive many ignites a discussion over what the disruption means. This discussion is necessarily political.

So another example: a crowd of white people confronting a Black man. Is this a lynch mob? Whites from the US South might have once tried, and some may still try, to say that this crowd is really citizens protecting their way of life. To the extent that anti-racist politics is successful, this kind of justification of violence registers as structural racism. In a racist context, though, the meaning of this crowd is contested; the disruption that the crowd produces incites an argument over whether it was a mob.

AB: *I was interested in the part of your book of "Left Individualism." Here you explore the fact that while individualism is associated with the Right, and even directly with Thatcherism, there is also a kind of individual identity, a kind of diversity of individuals, that is celebrated by the Left. I guess this is the somewhat crass idea that we are all beautiful and unique individuals and that we should welcome this milieu of diversity. Do you have any time for this idea, or is it just a neoliberalism that we ought to be wary of? You suggest that in order to be collectively influential, individualism needs to be thrown out entirely. Later in the book you write that collectivity is written off as undesirable by those who accuse it of "effacing difference." This is something I'd like to hear more about. Is it that right wing proponents of individualism use this "Left individualism" to prevent real collective action actually happening, to make us feel like unique individuals rather than a collective force?*

JD: After 1989, and, for some, after 1968, some on the Left became liberals. They acquiesced to the idea that there was no alternative to capitalism and put away the project of eliminating property, free markets, and commodity production. For a certain libertarian and/or liberal Left, the challenge of Leftist politics became one of securing freedoms from the state, freedoms of personal identity and creativity. Economic inequality is either ignored or flattened into just another issue. I say all this because the problem is not simply right-wing individualism. I say this because the Left took on too much of the right-wing individualist worldview. In the book, I explore this in various ways, one of which is the debate in *Marxism Today* in Britain. What you see is the jettisoning of collectivism and defense of individualism. Even for those defending some version of socialism or market regulation, the justification is individualist — the communist value of solidarity is displaced by the liberal prioritization of the individual.

AB: *I found myself interested in what your main theoretical influences are in this book. One theorist I want to talk about is Louis Althusser. You invert Althusser's concept of interpellation, and I think this is a very useful move. While Althusser claimed that individuals were interpellated from an undifferentiated mass of unique subjects and turned into a collective conformist population, you argue the opposite: that we are a collective mass who are interpellated into the condition of individual subjectivity. Could you explain why this reversed way of seeing ideology would help us see things different politically?*

JD: It lets us grasp very clearly the political damage inflicted by individualism. Collective strength becomes our default mode, something to encourage, amplify, and defend. Individual preference then appears as the way capitalism weakens us. I think most of us have been in protests where we feel the energy that comes from all of us together. We push up against barricades, sometimes breaking through fences or barriers. We feel invincible. The police weaken us as they pick us off, one by one, whether that happens at the moment of arrest or later in the process.

AB: *One last question, though I should make it clear that there is just a massive amount that we haven't covered in* Crowds and Party *and that they'll need to get it. As a Lacanian myself, it's this that I was most affected by in the book. What is "imitative mania," and how can we either get out of it or use it to do something decent politically?*

JD: One of my moves in the book is to try to take the features associated with crowds and make them positive. So, crowds tend to have distinctive ways of acting, described by classical crowd theorists and more contemporary empirical accounts of crowd phenomena in terms of bubbles, bandwagoning, "going viral." These include suggestibility, feelings of invincibility, and, as you mention, imitation, to mention but a few. Imitative mania refers to the way that people in crowds tend to imitate others. People like to do what others are doing. Easy examples might be chanting, singing, hand motions, "the wave." It also gets more intense when people show up in costumes, like say, *Star Wars* costumes for the opening of *Star Wars,* or *Harry Potter* costumes, and so on. Right now in the US you see people at Bernie Sanders's events dressing up like Bernie Sanders, or dressing their babies like Bernie. Some read this as a kind of adulation of the leader. That's clearly wrong. The so-called leader (Han Solo? Harry Potter?) doesn't know this is happening. The people do it for each other, demonstrating, I argue, the source of power comes from the crowd and that the object being imitated is just an opportunity for the crowd to express this power.

I think this idea can be useful for us politically because it can let us recognize leaders as just another object, just another opportunity like a slogan, hashtag, or image, that lets a crowd feel its energy.

6

GARETH BRANWYN
Borg Like Me

Interview and illustration by Roy Christopher
November 5, 2014

Over the past thirty-odd years, writer Gareth Branwyn has been amassing an impressive body of work on the fringes of cyberculture. He wrote for *bOING bOING* when it was still a print zine, did his own zine called *Going Gaga* before that, was an editor at *Mondo 2000, Wired, MAKE,* does book reviews for *WINK,* has edited over a dozen books, and is a regular contributor to my own Summer Reading Lists. He's stayed as jacked-in to our current technoculture as one can be, for as long as there's been a jack. His new book, *Borg Like Me & Other Tales of Art, Eros, and Embedded Systems* (Sparks of Fire Press, 2014), collects almost three hundred pages of his pieces from all over the place. It's like a cross between a very personal, edited collection on cyberpunk and a zine anthology.

The last time I interviewed Branwyn in 2001, he told me,

> one of the great things about being so bloody old is that I've had a chance to experience every flavor of fringe media from the mid-'70s on. I caught the tail end of '70s hippie media, then the punk DIY movement of the '80s, then the 'zine publishing scene of the '90s, and then web publishing in the '90s.

I finally met Gareth IRL at Maker Faire in Austin in 2008, and we haven't had a genuine sit-down in over ten years. Once I got my hands on a copy of *Borg Like Me*, I knew it was time to catch up with him again.

ROY CHRISTOPHER: *After all of these years, what finally prompted the collecting of all of these pieces?*

GARETH BRANWYN: This is a book I started putting together years ago, before I became the Editorial Director at MAKE. But that job was so all-consuming, I knew the book would never happen if I stayed there. So, I left early last year and immediately launched a Kickstarter campaign. I also thought I had a very fun and innovative idea for a collection of this kind, what I call a lazy man's memoir. I collected content from my thirty-plus-year career and then wove a new, personal narrative around it via deep intros to the pieces and new essays that helped flesh out the "story." These, hopefully, create a narrative arc and a point to this book that makes it more interesting, and far more personal, than just a collection of my best writing.

RC: *The title of the collection has a very personal connotation that people don't necessarily know about. Tell us about your very close relationship with the machine.*

GB: Well, as I like to tell people: I have an artificial hip, a rebuilt heart, and I take a biological drug that's bioengineered from mice proteins. So, I am literally a chimera — part man, part machine, part mouse. But as I make the point in the book, we are all so heavily mediated by technology and cutting-edge medical science at this point that we are all now cyborgs — part human, part machine.

The book's subtitle, *& Other Tales of Art, Eros, and Embedded Systems,* also reveals more than people may be aware about me. Over the course of my career, I've written about far more than technology. I've written a lot about art, music, relationships, and love, the occult and spirituality, and various aspects of underground media and culture. I even wrote a column for a sex magazine many years ago. This book is something of a coming out for me, revealing more about the breadth of my interests than I ever have before to a widespread audience. I'm like an onion, man. Layers.

RC: *You're primarily known as a writer through your writings on technology and technology-influenced cyberculture, yet you claim not to be that into technology. What gives, man?*

GB: Well, that subtitle was a little bit of an exaggeration for effect. I'm not in love with technology for technology's sake. I'm most fascinated by how people actually use technology and how they bend, and even break, it for their own purposes. As I say in the book, referring to the William Gibson quote "the street finds its own uses for things," I'm more interested in the street than the things. Because I've written extensively on how-to technology, such as robot building, people think of me as a real hacker, a real geek. But I'm not. Most of my geek/hacker friends like to tinker and problem solve tech for its own sake, for the challenge. I don't. I just want my tech to work. As I once said in a *MAKE* bio piece once: "I'm more of a puffy-sleeved romantic than a pocket-protected geek."

RC: *One of the images from* Jamming the Media *that has always stuck in my head is that of you and your then-four-year-old son Blake leaving the darkened room of blinking lights that was your media lab at the time. Tell us about his involvement in* Borg Like Me.

GB: That's from the introduction to *Jamming the Media,* a piece called "The Electronic Cottage: A Flash Forward." I included that in *Borg Like Me.* Because of my work in cutting-edge tech and media, Blake grew up completely immersed in early personal technology tools. They all came completely natural to him. He's a twenty-seven-year-old digital artist and game designer now, living in the Bay Area, and I think that early immersion is a reason why. He and I used to do things like create animated cartoons in HyperCard by drawing animation frames by hand, scanning them into the computer, and then creating crude animations by flipping the hypercards really fast. I think we even put music on some of them. And one of the games I got for review, *Creatures,* had a huge impact on him and made him declare he wanted to be a game designer. Hell, he even did some kid reviews of games and early LEGO Mindstorms in *Wired* and *The Baltimore Sun.* When he was a kid, I actually used to fantasize about him growing up and being some sort of artist, writer, or other creative type, and us collaborating on stuff. So it was a dream come true working together on this book. At one point, I joked that he was acting as my project manager. So we decided to make it official. He was very pro about it and really did help keep me on track. He also did a ton of incidental art, icons for the book and such, did animation elements for my Kickstarter video, and graphics for the KS campaign. He also co-designed the rubber stamps I created to accompany the book, which I use on all of the mailing envelopes and letters I send out. It really does feel like the book was a collaboration between us. There were so many deeply gratifying aspects of doing this book. Working with him was definitely a highlight.

The book was also something of a "getting the band back together." I worked with eighteen artists from my old zine and early cyberculture mag days, people like Mark Frauenfelder, Danny Hellman, John Bergin, Shannon Wheeler, William Braker. There are thirty-some illustrations in all.

RC: *The artwork was the next thing I was going to ask about. You beat me to it: twenty years ago, you wrote that "hackers represent the scouts to a new territory that is just now beginning to be mapped out by others." How would you adjust or amend your conception of the hacker since?*

GB: Well, the territory has certainly been mapped and settled and over-developed, and large tracts of it sold to the highest bidder. I've told people at several of my talks recently that, in the 1990s when I was writing about the "frontier towns of cyberspace," I never for a moment could have imagined that my parents would now spend almost as much time online as I do. They are the most un-techie people I could imagine, and yet they have his and hers desktop computers, laptops, smart phones, and at least one tablet. But I think that "hacking the future" process is still happening. I was on a panel at SXSW this year, with Bruce Sterling, Cory Doctorow, and Chris Brown. The subject was basically, what happened to the cyberpunks? Sterling focused on the darker side of things, as he is wont to do: the Silk Road busts, Cody Wilson and 3D-printed guns, Eastern European cybercriminals, and the like. While I think that's all relevant, I argued that I think lots of cyberpunks became makers. A lot of the people I worked with at *MAKE* were very involved in early-'90s cyberculture. I think, for many of us, we got tired of the overemphasis on virtuality, hyper-mentality, and the denigration of "the meat," and so there was something of a corrective swing back towards physicality, getting your hands dirty. Mark Frauenfelder at *bOING bOING* has an interesting theory about this. In the '90s, when everyone was hacking software and the net, to share your work, all you had to do was send a file or link. But as soon as microcontrollers and other physical computing hardware became readily available and people started hacking with that, suddenly, you needed to show your work off in person. From this grew hardware meetups, hackerspaces, Maker Faires, and the like.

These days, when net neutrality is at stake, it's good to be reminded of the promise and potential that all of this networked tech initially offered.

One of the frequent takeaways from *Borg Like Me* that I've heard from readers is that, in the essays about early cyberculture, there's a palpable sense of frontier spirit, passion, and a sense of just how powerful and potentially revolutionary these democratizing tools can be. These days, when net neutrality is at stake, it's good to be reminded of the promise and potential that all of this networked tech initially offered. Sure the techno-cultural changes have been deep, and in many ways profound — we take for granted the power of that globally connected device that we carry, forgotten, in our pockets — but the drift towards mundanity and big media subsumption is insidious and steady. If the "you know, back when I was a cyberpunk..." stories in my book can inspire today's mutant change agents in even the smallest ways, I'd be thrilled.

RC: *Music is another deep interest we have in common. I love the "Immersive Media Notes" spread throughout the book. Diving into media headlong while writing is something I advocate regularly. Do you have specific "writing music," or do you play whatever you're into at the time?*

GB: Music has always been so deeply interwoven into my life, even before I met my late-wife, a musician, and lived with her for twenty-two years. I can't think of many things in my past without thinking of the music that soundtracked those experiences. As I was writing the book, I noticed how many pieces mentioned music, were about music, or had music attached to them in my mind. So I created those "Immersive Media Notes" so that readers could listen to the music associated with that piece before, during, or after. The idea was inspired by the essay "By This River" and the Eno song from where it gets its name. That song is so hauntingly beautiful to me and completely encodes much of my relationship with my wife. I felt like people *had* to listen to that track to better appreciate the feelings I was trying to convey in that piece. It's funny though: I actually added the "Immersive Media Notes" at the very last minute, even after the book was in first proofs, and it's one of the things that always gets mentioned by readers and reviewers.

RC: *What's coming up next for a* Borg Like You?

GB: I'm working on a number of projects. For my imprint,

Sparks of Fire Press, I'm working on two new chapbooks in the *Borg Like Me* series. The Eros Part is a collection of my writings on love, sex, and muses. I promised this as one of the premiums for my Kickstarter campaign. Then I'm working on a follow up to my popular *Gareth's Tips* on *Sucks-Less Writing*. I'm excited about that. I think there is some great new material in there. I'm also working on a big project I'm not at liberty to talk about, but if it comes through, it'll be amazing. Oh, and I've also been working on *Café Gaga,* which'll be a periodic podcast of things that are currently holding my attention. And I continue to do regular reviews for WINK *Books,* a gig that I really love. So, I'm definitely keeping busy!

7

IAN BOGOST
Worthwhile Dilemmas

Interview and illustration by Roy Christopher
July 3, 2012

Partially fueled by Jane McGonigal's bestselling *Reality Is Broken* (Penguin Books, 2011), "gamification" — turning mostly menial tasks into games through a system of points and rewards — became the buzzword of 2011 and diluted and/or stigmatized videogame studies on many fronts. Gaming ungamed situations is not all bad though. Brian Eno and Peter Schmidt's *Oblique Strategies* (1975) were tactics for gaming a stalled creative process. In an interview with Steven Johnson, Brian Eno explained, "the trick for me isn't about showing people how to be creative as though they've never been like that before, but rather trying to find ways of recontacting the natural playfulness and curiosity that most people were born with." When it becomes exploitative, it becomes a problem.

Enter one of the most outspoken, prolific, and creative videogame scholars working today. Ian Bogost is a professor at Georgia Tech and co-founded videogame design company, Persuasive Games. Among his many books are *Unit Operations: An Approach to Videogame Criticism* (MIT Press, 2008), *Persuasive Games: The Expressive Power of Videogames* (MIT Press, 2010), and *How to Do Things with Videogames* (University of Minnesota Press, 2011), as well as *A Slow Year: Game Poems* (Open Texture, 2010), the latter of which includes four videogames and many meditative poems about the Atari 2600. His latest is *Alien Phenomenology, or What It's Like to Be a Thing* (University of Minnesota Press, 2012), which calls for an object-oriented approach to things as things and for thinkers to also become makers.

ROY CHRISTOPHER: *While reading* How to Do Things with Videogames, *it occurred to me that videogames really are the medium of the now. They encompass so much of everything else our media does and is. Was this part of your point, and I just need a late pass?*

IAN BOGOST: Maybe it would be more accurate to say that videogames are the least recognized medium of the now. In the book, in the first chapter even, I argue against the conceit that games have not achieved their potential. That's true of course, but what medium has achieved its potential? But in that context, I was speaking against researchers, critics, and designers who talk about everything videogames are not, but could be — akin to film, or novels, or textbooks, or what have you. The book tries to show that videogames are already a great many things, from art to pornography to work to exercise.

But all that said, videogames are hardly a dominant medium. What is instead? Some might say "the internet," but that's wrong too, although the reasons it is wrong are surprising. As Marshall McLuhan taught us, media contain other media. But weirdly, even though we access the internet on computers, the former actually has relatively little to do with the latter. The internet contains writing, images, moving images, sound — all "traditional" media in common parlance. McLuhan's idea of the Global Village was meant to rekindle the senses overlooked thanks to the age of print, and in that sense TV and the internet have succeeded in realizing that vision. But the result turns out to be just the same as TV and radio and print, except any of us can create the equivalent of a publisher or a broadcaster.

Videogames, by contrast, have different properties than these other media. They model the way something works rather than describing or showing it; they offer an experience of making choices within that model rather than an audiovisual replay of it; and they contextualize that model within the context of a simulated world. Now, to be sure, that sort of approach is very "now" in the sense that we should be interested in the complex, paradoxical interrelations of the moving parts in a system. But at the end of the day, it's just easier to watch cat videos on YouTube and spout one-liners onto Twitter. In some sense, videogames both are and aren't other media. They do what other media do — and some things they do not — but they do them differently.

RC: *The idea of attaching rewards to menial tasks is understandable, but the current buzz around gamification seems to miss much of the point by filtering out what's actually good about games. You've been quite vocal about the ills of this trend. What are we to do?*

IB: If videogames both have and haven't arrived as a mature medium, then the proponents of gamification want to pretend that the work is done and now we can settle into the task of counting the profits. The basics of this phenomenon are simple enough: marketers and consultants need to surf from trend to trend, and videogames are appealing and seductive but complex and misunderstood, so the simple directive to apply incentives to all our experiences both satisfies the economic rationalists and ticks off the "game strategy" box for organizations.

The irony, not lost on many, is that as virtual incentives like points and reward programs have risen, so tangible incentives have gone into decline. We used to provide material incentives in the form of things like compensation, benefits, perks, and so forth. Now we use JPEGs and 32-bit integers.

In fact, just as I was writing this response, a friend told me about a novella someone wrote that appears to be an introduction to gamification. It's called "I'll Eat This Cricket for a Cricket Badge," written by a marketing consultant with the improbably parodic-sounding name Darren Steele. The description reads, "this is the story of Lara, a senior director at Albatron Global. Today she learns she has 24 hours to prepare for a once-in-a-decade meeting with 'The Brotherhood,' the triumvirate of terror that founded the company." Imagine if these gamification shills spent even a fraction of the energy and creativity they devote to swindling on the earnest implementation of worthwhile ideas. In fact, I can't even tell if the novella is serious or not, the world has become that ambiguous.

As with most things, knowing what to do about it is harder, thanks to mere critique. And in that respect, it's always dangerous to fight against marketers and consultants. Though often stupid, they are also very smart. Or, better yet, they often use their savvy to appear stupid or simplistic so that we'll let them into our homes and our minds.

In that respect, one possible strategy of opposition is to infiltrate the consultancies and corporations themselves; to create our own highly leveraged solutions-oriented roll-out for it-doesn't-matter-what service. It's too laborious and time-consuming to convince people to make games in earnest, so to combat gamification we need to seed a distraction, a new trend that will dissipate this one. Media theory as consultancy counter-terrorism.

RC: *A set of tactics like Brian Eno and Peter Schmidt's* Oblique Strategies *seems a better tack for bringing gaming ideas into other areas of creative problem solving.*

IB: Eno and Schmidt's *Oblique Strategies* were originally meant to spur ideas for artists, but now we see similar idea cards being used in design and business too, and the famous design firm IDEO released something similar a few years back. And given our Facebook-status-oriented and Twitterified media ecosystem, there seems to be a strong interest in aphoristic world views. And for that matter, Jesse Schell developed a series of cards around his theory of game design, which he calls "lenses" in a textbook called *The Art of Game Design*. So, there are some precedents for bits-and-pieces idea generation around games.

But there's a chicken-egg problem at work here too. In order to be susceptible to the surprising solutions of idea generation, you still have to be conversant enough in those ideas to give them life. For example, many of the phrases on the original *Oblique Strategies* cards are meant for musicians, the deck's original creative context, and if you are not a musician, it's hard to imagine understanding how to "mute and continue" or "left channel, right channel, center channel" unless you were already well-versed in musical concepts. Admittedly, these are pretty basic ideas, basic enough that even a layperson can grasp them, but that's only because the experience of recorded music is so universal. The basics are shared as a literacy. But that literacy had to come from somewhere, and, until the literacy is developed for games, design tools for their increased application will remain mired in ignorance. To use games, we must know games, but to know them we must have used them.

This is why progress will be stochastic. In *How to Do Things with Videogames* I argue that games will have arrived through incremental examples altering, increasing, changing our ideas of what games can do. I didn't use this language there, but it's a kind of accretion, in which the medium grows bit by bit over time, eventually developing a larger and larger gravity. This process is both recursive and compounded, in the sense that individual successes feedback on our overall comfort and knowledge, becoming candidates for the kind of idea generation that *Oblique Strategies* exemplifies.

RC: Cow Clicker *is like your hit song that won't stop playing. People's missing the point seemed to prove its point further. Even with its persistence, did you accomplish what you set out to do?*

IB: *Cow Clicker* is so much bigger than me now, it's not even possible to know if it did what I set out for it to do, or if that's even a desirable outcome. There's an internet adage called Poe's Law that says that it's often difficult or even impossible to tell the difference between extremism and its parody. It was originally coined in relation to discussions of evolution within Christian forums, but it's been generalized since — a parody of something extreme can be mistaken for the real thing. And if a real thing sounds sufficiently extreme, it can be mistaken for parody.

The best example of this phenomenon these days is *The Onion*. There's a whole website, literallyunbelievable.org, that collects reactions from readers who mistake Onion articles for the real deal, such as the fuming reactions from folks who took seriously headlines like "Planned Parenthood Opens $8 Billion Abortionplex." And then on the flip side, it's become common to hear people say of undeniably real headlines, "is this an *Onion* article?" The lines between reality and absurdity have blended.

So, it's clear that *Cow Clicker* is far weirder than my original intentions. Rather than reflect more on whether or not I succeeded, I've started asking other questions. What happened? is certainly one of them, and I'm not sure I'll ever wrap my head around it. Perhaps more interesting: what can I learn from it? or even, what's next for *Cow Clicker*? The latter question just terrifies me, because I've tried so hard to distance myself from the madness that running the game entailed. But it's also short-sighted. After all, *Cow Clicker* was popular. It still is. People like clicking on cows! What can I do with that observation? What can I make that takes that lesson in a direction unburdened by the concerns of obsession and enframing? Is it even possible? In any case, I'm not giving anything away when I say that I don't think I'm done with *Cow Clicker* yet. Or, better, I don't think *Cow Clicker* is done with me.

RC: *Videogames inform most of your work, including your new title,* Alien Phenomenology. *Tell us about your foray into object-oriented ontology and its link with videogames.*

IB: Object-oriented ontology seems like an obvious match for media studies. Any scholar or creator of media interested in the "thingness" of their objects of study has something to gain from OOO. In addition to, or even instead of, studies of political economy and reception, we can add studies of the material history and construction of computational devices. In other words, "materialism" need not retail only its Marxist sense but also its realist one: not just political economy but also just stuff.

I suspected there would be productive connections with object-oriented philosophy, and I remember waiting for Graham Harman's *Tool-Being: Heidegger and the Metaphysics of Objects* (Open Court) to be published in 2002 so I could read it and apply it in my dissertation. I'd been following the emergence and growth of speculative realism with interest, but from afar.

Then two things happened. First, I started thinking about the idea of a "pragmatic" speculative realism, one that would embrace some of the first principles devised by the movements' true philosophers, but that would put them to use in the service of specific objects but looking beyond human experience. That thought was in my head since 2005 or so.

The second thing was the Atari. Several years ago, I learned how to program the 1977 Atari Video Computer System (VCS), the console that made home videogame play popular. Nick Montfort and I were working on a book on the platform, *Racing the Beam* (MIT Press, 2009), about the relationship between the hardware design of the Atari VCS and the creative practices that its designers and programmers invented in those early days of the videogame. The Atari featured a truly unique custom graphics and sound chip called the Television Interface Adapter (TIA). It made bizarre demands on game makers. Instead of preparing a screen's worth of television picture all at once, the programmer had to make changes to the data the TIA sent to the television in tandem with the scanline-by-scanline movement of the television's electron beam. Programming the Atari feels more like plowing a field than like drawing a picture.

As I became more and more familiar with this strange system, I couldn't help but feel enchanted by its parts as much as its output. Sure, the Atari was made by people in order to entertain other people, and, in that sense, it's just a machine. But a machine and its components are also something more, something alive, almost. I found myself asking, what is it like to be an Atari, or a Television Interface Adapater, or a cathode ray tube television? The combination of that media-specific call to action and my broader interest in object-oriented ontology more generally catalyzed the project that became *Alien Phenomenology,* a book about using speculation to understand the experience of things, of what it's like to be a thing.

RC: *What's coming up next for you?*

IB: There's a concept in sales, the "sales funnel." It's a structured approach to selling products and services that helps salespeople move opportunities from initial contact through closing by structuring that process in a number of elements. Those might include securing leads, validating leads, identifying needs, qualifying prospects, developing proposals, negotiating, closing the sale, of course, and then managing and retaining the client.

In sales, it's always best to keep the contacts and leads elements at the top of the funnel very full because those opportunities will winnow away through attrition, disinterest, loss, and other factors. You tend to have far fewer proposals and negotiations than you do contacts.

I often think about my upcoming creative work through a similar kind of structure. The "creative funnel," we might call it. We can even use some of the same language: leads, opportunities, commitments, publishing, and support, or something like that. In any case, I tend to throw a whole lot of stuff at the wall — lead and opportunities — because I know that far fewer of those ideas will actually be realized.

In the leads and opportunities column, I'm currently working with my co-editor Nick Montfort to support a number of new books in the Platform Studies series, the series we began with *Racing the Beam.* Those include both popular and esoteric game consoles and microcomputers. As for my own writing, I'm trying to identify which of a number of books I'll pursue next. I've got one planned on game criticism, a series of critical pieces on specific games, one on games and sports, one on Apple, a book on McLuhan and metaphysics with Levi Byrant, the crazy kernel of a follow-up to *Alien Phenomenology*, and a book on play that I would call my attempt at a Malcolm Gladwell-style trade book. Who knows which, if any, of those will ever come to fruition.

As for commitments, Levi and I are finishing a collection called *New Realisms and Materialisms*, which we hope will paint a very broad portrait of the different ways of thinking that take those names, applied to a variety of domains, from philosophy to art, architecture to ecology. I'm also desperate to make some new games. I've got a small iOS puzzle game in the works, and a larger, weirder piece that should open at the Jacksonville Museum of Contemporary Art in the fall of 2012 and see a general release shortly thereafter.

And I'm closing, if you will, on a big game infrastructure project, the *Game-O-Matic* authoring system. It was funded by the Knight Foundation two years ago as a tool to help journalists quickly and easily make games about current events without specialized game-design or programming knowledge, and it's just about to release into beta. The system is sort of magical: it takes a concept map — a diagram of nouns with verbs connecting them — and turns them into a playable game. Folks can sign up to use it for free.

I'm currently struggling to take seriously my own idea of "carpentry," the practice of making things that do theory described in *Alien Phenomenology*. I'm trying to expand my theoretical output beyond books, but I still love reading and writing, so I hope I'll end up with an interesting menagerie of new, little creatures over the next few years.

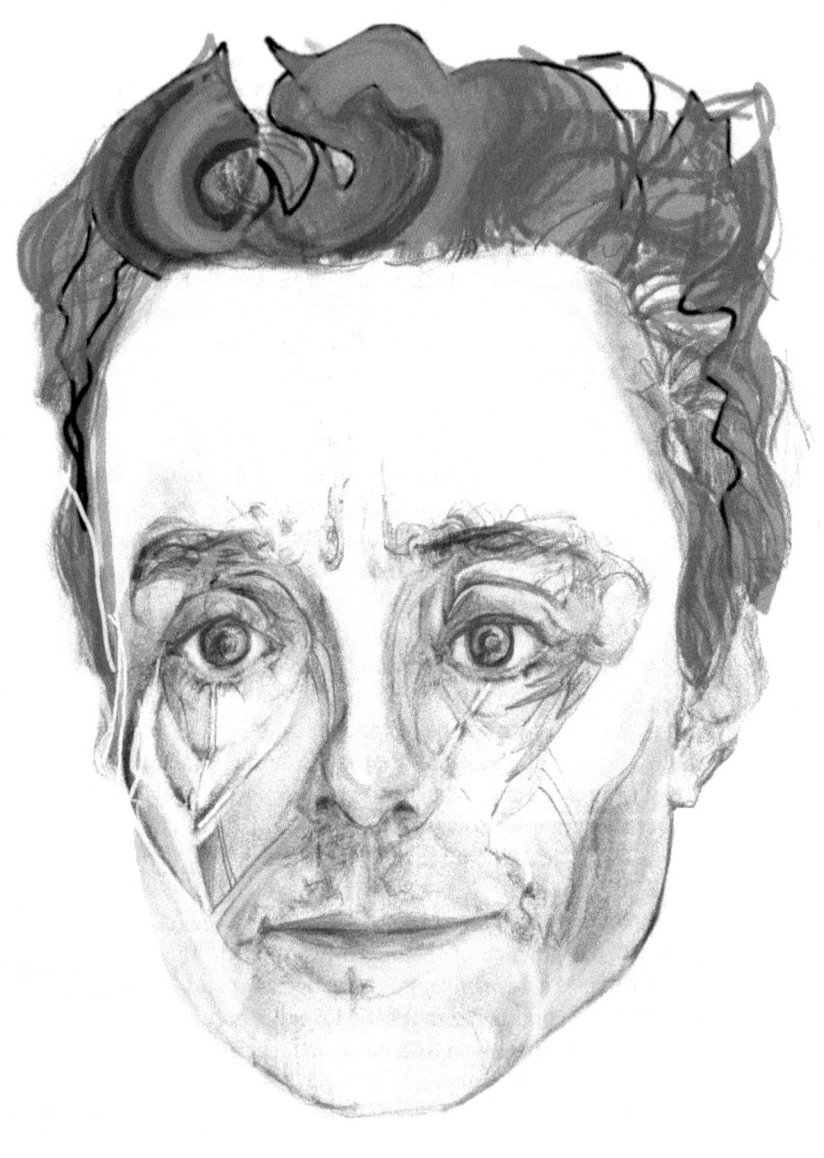

8

MARK DERY
Nothing's Shocking

Interview by Roy Christopher
Illustration by Eleanor Purcell
March 29, 2012

I read a review of a Weird Al Yankovich record several years ago (i.e., eons past Al's 1980s prime) that pointed out that his schtick had become commonplace. When irony and parody become the norm, the edges move toward the middle. When culture jamming becomes culture, there's nothing left to jam. When the news is just another reality show… After many binges on the fringes, learning the edge, culture jamming, and cyberpunking during the 1990s, chronicled in his books *Culture Jamming* (OpenMedia, 1993), *Flame Wars* (Duke University Press, 1994), *Escape Velocity* (Grove Press, 1996), and *The Pyrotechnic Insanitarium* (Grove Press, 1999), Mark Dery is back with a collection of essays from the meantime, *I Must Not Think Bad Thoughts: Drive-by Essays on American Dread, American Dreams* (University of Minnesota Press, 2012). It's been twelve years since our last virtual sit-down, so I thought it was time to check in again.

I cracked open Dery's first book in over a decade and landed on the story about blogging, which, with an adept analysis of all-over-the-map, curiosity-collecting blogs like *bOING bOING*, explains further the plight of cultural criticism as Dery does it. Realizing I was getting ahead of myself, I backed up to Bruce Sterling's foreword, which coincidentally references the one piece I'd read. "This is prescience in conditions of historical inevitability," Sterling writes about Dery's blog piece in "World Wide Wonder Closet: On Blogging": "I learn useful things like this by paying close attention to Mark Dery—not just to his writings, mind you, but to his career." Dery describes the situation himself, writing in 2003:

> years of tabloid media, reality TV, attacking heads, and, more recently, nightly news nightmares of doomed workers leaping from the World Trade Center, hand in hand, or journalists beheaded in your living room by jihadi or the slapstick torture at Abu Ghraib—home movies from hell that employed the visual grammar of porn—have cauterized our cultural nerve endings. Little wonder, then, that ever greater subcultural voltages are needed to shock us.

The same laser-focused interrogation and machete-sharp wit that made Dery's earlier books critical touchstones is here in rapid-fire form. Where his earlier work honed in on one subject or one genre of subjects, *I Must Not Think Bad Thoughts* is all over the place, a sniper-perch on the cultural sprawl where no one and nothing is safe. There are too many stand-out, entrails-examining moments to name, but his outing of HAL 9000 in "Straight, Gay, or Binary: HAL Comes out of the Cybernetic Closet" is likely to become one of the most talked-about essays. No matter the topic, no one puts together a sentence like Mark Dery.

Appropriately, I believe, Dery's next project is a biography of gothic artist and writer Edward Gorey for Little, Brown & Co. but I'll let him tell you about that.

ROY CHRISTOPHER: *Not to be impertinent from the beginning, but where have you been?*

MARK DERY: Impertinence will get you everywhere. In 1999 I published *The Pyrotechnic Insanitarium: American Culture on the Brink,* a portrait of fin-de-millennium America — paranoid, violent, economically stratified, ideologically polarized, demographically balkanized — as reflected in cultural phenomena that hyperbolized the zeitgeist: Timothy McVeigh, the Unabomber, the Heaven's Gate cult, dug-in survivalists, fear-sick suburbanites circling the wagons in gated communities, jittery celebrities installing secret "safe rooms" in their mansions, Disney's experiment in privatized governance and white-picket nostalgia (Celebration, Florida), apparitions of the evil clown in our media dream life, and the branding of everything, ourselves included. Like *Escape Velocity* before it, it was generally well-received, critically, although it suffered some critical brickbats, most notably from Pre-Cambrian feminist and professional bean-counter Elaine Showalter, who tallied up my references to women's issues (whatever those are) and found the book wanting, and Michiko Kakutani at the *Times,* who had a fit of the vapors over my tendency to name-check Donna Haraway, which upsets the mental digestion of the paper's readers.

But, contrary to popular belief, the rich pickings of the writing life fall somewhat short of a hedge-fund manager's annual bonus, so I joined the professoriat, teaching courses in creative nonfiction ("The Popular Essay") and media theory ("Reading the Media") in the Department of Journalism at New York University. I toiled in the fields of corporate academe until 2009, when I returned to writing full-time. Teaching has its rewards, chief among them the privilege of rubbing brains with some of the brightest minds around and the unimaginably gratifying experience of hearing former students confess some small debt of gratitude for the writerly wisdom you've imparted. And it has its more dubious pleasures, notably: faculty meetings, committee meetings, the territorial threat-displays of colleagues of very small brain, and the scenery-chewing hysterics of my department's resident diva, an aspiring Sontag who dyed her hair an unconvincing magenta and who, in dead seriousness, once compared the department prohibition on holding her class in a communal study room to Nazi regulations in the Warsaw ghetto. Oh, and seeing yourself compared, on some *RateYourProfessors*-type site, to Snape. (Actually, that last was pure awesome, since Snape is my favorite character in the Potter movies — the only thing that makes them watchable, really. I'm always rooting for him.) In all seriousness, though, I couldn't manage the trick of balancing the demands of classroom and writing desk. Some of my former colleagues were brilliant in the classroom and productive as writers; I respect them immensely. But teaching ate me up, leaving little time or energy for my writing. And, since my writing is at the heart of my sense of myself — it's not just what I do, but who I am — there came a point when I had to choose between the financial security of an academic sinecure and the less tangible rewards of the writing life. Full disclosure demands that I say, too, that the politics of the institution conspired against me, but I'll spare you the petty details of academic bloodletting. Anyway, I'm happy to be back where I belong, scribbling for a living.

RC: *Since your books in the 1990s, the odd subjects you covered then have become the everyday. Where does that shift leave your current work? Are you headed further out into the cultural hinterlands?*

MD: Well, it leaves *The Pyrotechnic Insanitarium* looking eerily prescient, I'm immodest enough to point out. I've been gratified by posts by apparently young readers, on GoodReads and Amazon, noting how contemporary that book feels. For example, the free-floating paranoia and anti-government conspiracy theories and anti-immigrant nativism of the '90s militia movement is alive and well in the Tea Party and out on the survivalist fringe. As well, that late-'90s sense of American mass culture as a media-mad Tilt-a-Whirl spinning out of control, and of American society as a place where the center cannot hold and the worst are full of passionate intensity, is still with us, although it waxes and wanes, to be sure.

I Must Not Think Bad Thoughts collects essays from the past decade or so, and, in a plot twist I never would have imagined, some of the more recent pieces mark a turn toward a more personal style, by which I do not mean what back-of-the-magazine American essayists typically mean, which is soppy confessionalism, but rather the use of myself as a prism for refracting the cultural dynamics and historical events around me, as, say, Montaigne did in *Essais* or Didion did in *The White Album* or Luc Sante does in *Kill Your Darlings* or Richard Rodriguez does in nearly all of his books. So, I'm lighting out for the territories within as a way of making deeper sense of American dread and American dreams, to quote the book's subtitle.

RC: *Unlike other books of its kind,* I Must Not Think Bad Thoughts *is a strangely cohesive examination of America's viscera over the past fifteen years or so. How much of it was written with the collection in mind?*

MD: None of it. Each essay was what McLuhan would call a probe — a nomadic rover, wound up and let loose on the terrain of a media event, a cultural trend, an idea whose time has come, a historical premonition of our moment, the collective unconscious of America, whatever. But as its subtitle, *Drive-by Essays,* suggests, it's an armchair version of the philosophical travelog, a tradition that stretches from de Tocqueville to Henry Miller's *Air-Conditioned Nightmare* to Baudrillard's *America* to Bernard-Henri Lévy's *American Vertigo.*

RC: *Tell me about the next book project. It seems a perfect pairing of subject and sensibility.*

MD: It's a biography of the writer, illustrator, and inimitable eccentric Edward Gorey. More than that I can't say, since it's still in the research stage. I haven't put pen to paper but must start soon, since I've got to deliver the manuscript sometime next year. Just saying that — "sometime next year" — inspires a thrill of terror so debilitating I may have to go lie down for a while, with a cold compress on my forehead.

RC: *What else is coming up?*

MD: I've just contributed a short essay to *Hidden Treasure* (Blast Books, 2012), an incomparably beautiful compendium "showcasing astonishing and rare" oddities and arcana from the National Library of Medicine: chromolithographs from the *Atlas of Skin Diseases,* magic lantern slides, *Stereoscopic Pictures for Cross-Eyed Children,* Health and Hygiene Puzzle Blocks from the Number 10 Shanghai Toy Factory in 1960s "Red China," an 1839 lithograph illustrating the postmortem examination of a man(?) with sexually ambiguous genitalia, a 1924 German tract extolling the virtues of nudism. It's a simply breathtaking, a cabinet of wonders between two covers: 450 unforgettable images, accompanied by brief essays, ranging over the intimately alien landscapes of bodies rendered monstrous by injury, disease, or congenital deformity. Also, I've got a personal essay-cum-cultural critique of the Rorschach test in the works for *The Believer,* something for *The Awl* on *Young Americans*-era David Bowie as "white negro" and "postmodern minstrel," and an essay on the future of the human body for a museum exhibition catalog.

9

BRIAN ENO
Strange Overtones

Interview by Steven Johnson
Illustration by Roy Christopher
October 4, 2011

Brian Eno is a musician, producer, artist, writer, and technologist whose ideas have had an astonishingly wide impact on our culture since the early 1970s. His solo and collaborative records with artists like David Byrne and John Cale have helped inaugurate new genres of music, including ambient generative music, as well as pioneering techniques that became essential to modern sampling. As a producer, he has a long track record of creating essential new sounds with some of the most famous musicians in the world: David Bowie, the Talking Heads, U2, and Coldplay. His art installations have been showcased at locations around the world, and he has even collaborated with the game designer Will Wright to create the generative soundtrack for the game Spore.

STEVEN JOHNSON: *I'm looking at this card deck of Oblique Strategies that you created with Peter Schmidt many years ago, and the little introduction to the set says the cards arose out of "observations of the principles underlying what we were doing." So, I guess that's where I want to start: you've had this extraordinarily* *innovative career in multiple fields. Do you see some underlying principles behind the way you have come upon new ideas?*

BRIAN ENO: Anyone who's had children will know that the urge to create — to make something from nothing — is innate. You can't stop kids from doing it: they're perpetually inventing. Sometimes we manage, through our education systems, to multiply that energy. Often we manage to stifle it. The trick for me isn't about showing people how to be creative as though they've never been like that before but rather trying to find ways of recontacting the natural playfulness and curiosity that most people were born with. There are quite a few facets to this, but a very big part of it involves moving away from the idea that "creativity" is an exclusively individual thing, that it springs up in certain gifted individuals, entirely from their imaginations. The more you look at the history of art and science, the more you notice that it is as much to do with the contingencies of the time — the technologies that were around, the conversations that were taking place, and so on. This isn't to say that there are no differences between minds but rather that those differences might be of another order than pure "processing power." They might have a lot to do with the sheer luck of where you happened to be born, of who said what and when, of what tools were available to you.

I think one thing that we don't normally acknowledge is the power of our tools and technologies. We like to imagine that ideas pop fully formed out of our minds as the result of our internal, creative processes. And we imagine that we then create the technologies we use in order to realize those creative flashes. So, classically, a scientist has a theory and devises an experimental apparatus to test it. Although this does sometimes happen, I think more often it's the reverse that takes place — that it's the technology that precedes the understanding of the principles. This happens in science a lot. A tool is invented, and the tool then leads to some new realization, something that you could now do or see or understand that you could never have understood before. I think that very often happens in the arts. My favorite example, because it's the one I've spent my life working with, is the recording studio. The multitrack studio was invented for completely mundane reasons so that engineers could more easily balance the vocalist against the rest of the performers. They didn't have to make those critical decisions before the recording; they could do it afterward. But of course, that humble invention gave rise to a whole different way of making music, really a completely different understanding of music.

So, in my particular case, a lot of my creative behavior has come from looking at technologies, new tools, and thinking, "you know what, this allows you to do something that nobody ever thought to do before."

SJ: *Is there a process for that? How do you explore a new piece of technology?*

BE: I spend a fair amount of my time just fiddling around listening for something new. I'm always fascinated when I hear something I haven't heard before and think, "wow, nobody's ever done that before." And sometimes I think, "nobody's ever done that before — but it's fantastic! If I don't get it out quickly, somebody else is going to discover it very shortly." [Laughs.] So my process — you could call it noodling, really — it's just playing with the materials, trying to understand where we are now that we weren't yesterday. That's how the idea for *Discreet Music* came about. It was a very simple discovery that if you connected together two tape recorders in a particular way you could create a very long delay, so that the echo of something comes back five or six seconds after you've played it, then you can play on top of it; and then you can play on top of the two of them, and the three of them. So, you can build up dense layers of material in real time. One person becomes an orchestra. But you could never do that before. The possibility arises entirely out of the technology of tape recorders.

In fact, the funny thing about *Discreet Music* is that I first did it with three recorders, and it took me months to realize that I only needed two! I don't know why but I had these three recorders in a row, and I had two playbacks and one record, and that's how I used it for a long time. And it was at least months, possibly years, before I realized, "you know what, I don't need that third recorder." [Laughs.] It was very funny. It had been like magic the first time I did it, so I never questioned the format.

SJ: *One other interesting thing about your career is that you've had such a big influence as a producer, in a sense coaxing new musical ideas out of other people. What strategies have you developed in that kind of context?*

BE: First of all, the very fact of having somebody who isn't in the band and who is suggesting new ways of working is in itself very powerful. Because that person is not part of the political/diplomatic situation within the band itself. You know, any band that's been together for a very long time has done it partly by being polite to one another; a certain level of decent human rapport. So, it's very difficult within a band if somebody does something and you don't think it's a very good idea. It's still quite hard to say, "look, that's no good. Let's not bother with that." You're duty-bound to go through the process of exploring it until the person himself says, "yeah, it's not that good is it?" Whereas having somebody from the outside coming and looking at a piece without any particular loyalties or prejudices and saying, "well, that's working, but I don't think this is working. And this bit over here could work…" People are much more ready to accept an assessment like that from somebody that they know is not personally engaged in the work. So, the producer as outsider just in itself is important.

Also, the fact of having to present things to somebody, which is what a band is doing when they're talking to a producer, means that they have to articulate and package the thing, if you like. They have to bring it to some kind of position where somebody else can look at it. It has to be more than a vague idea. So, I think it encourages the band to focus on what they're doing.

For instance, if I work with someone, and I say that I'll be in next Monday and maybe we can have a look at these pieces then. And just doing that makes the band say, "okay, we've got about fourteen guitars on that one. We should really sort out which ones we want to use before Brian comes along to hear it." So, the producer can be the person who catalyzes certain conclusions along the way, who says, "okay, where is this thing at now — how does it really stand at the moment?"

SJ: *We've talked before about your technique of having the members of the band play one another's instruments in the studio. I love that idea.*

BE: One of the other things that a producer can do is to think of ways to get people out of their habits. Any group of people who has worked together for a long period of time tends to fall into habits about how things are done. One person always tends to be the person who leads the process; another is the one who supports the leader; another, the one who comes in late and who doesn't say much until the very end; and another one is the stubborn one, counterbalancing the enthusiastic one. And that's all fine, that's part of the chemistry of a group of people working together. But it gets very habitual, and it gets quite boring, so I think of ways of upsetting that, turning it into a game actually. So, saying today, "you are going to give all the orders; and you, the person who normally does all the talking, you're going to just do what you're told. And you are going to play this instrument that you normally don't ever touch and, in fact, that you can't play." [Laughs.] So, sometimes that does actually yield an immediately usable result. But what does very often happen is that it loosens people up. And it enlarges the envelope of possibilities within which they navigate. I mean, if you tell somebody else to play drums, you have a very simple drumbeat normally because the person who has taken over the drums isn't the drummer, and, therefore, you start writing and thinking in a different way. It just immediately takes you out of the normal course you would have followed.

SJ: *I would think that recording in different cities, which you've often done, would be helpful in the same way — you're deliberately disorienting yourself with some new culture. I mean, I sometimes hear about people recording a record in some exotic place, and I think, "why are they traveling all the way there when they can just record it at home?"*

BE: I think one of the other reasons is simply that: getting away from home. So, you're not engaged with picking up the laundry and doing all the normal things for your everyday life. There's nothing else to do except what you're there to do. And I think that really helps a lot. It's the strongest reason for going someplace else. The location is almost irrelevant. What's more relevant is the fact that it's not your normal location.

SJ: *As you look over your career, are there periods where you see an unusual cluster of new ideas, where you just feel like you're on some kind of streak? And then are there fallow periods where nothing is really working?*

BE: I think there are periods that, when you're in them, seem desperately unfruitful, and you think, "why am I doing this? I'm completely useless, and I've lost it all." Then an idea finally strikes you, and you suddenly realize that you've been working on it for quite a long time, but you weren't aware of it. You've assembled all of the mental and physical tools you need to handle it in what seemed like a fallow period. So, I don't really believe in fallow periods anymore. I just think there are periods when you're aware that things are happening and then other periods where things are happening, but you're just not aware of them. There's a lot of time when I just don't know what I'm doing. I was talking to Laurie Anderson the other day. She's on tour and she phoned me, and I said, "do you sometimes wonder why we're all still doing this?" When I look back over my life and think about the times when I felt absolutely confident about what I was doing — it's probably about twenty periods of fifteen minutes or a half hour each, where I suddenly thought, "I know exactly what I'm doing now. I know what this is for; I know what I've been doing; I know what I'm about to do." It's a fantastic feeling and it gives you the energy to keep going for a very long time; because it only lasts a few minutes, before all the — not difficulties really — the ambiguities of the situation become evident.

10

ZIZI PAPACHARISSI
A Networked Self

Interview and illustration by Roy Christopher
April 17, 2011

Zizi Papacharissi is an academic powerhouse. Whatever you've been doing for the last fifteen years, she probably makes you look lazy. She holds a PhD in Journalism from my own University of Texas at Austin, an MA in Communication Studies from Kent State University, and a BA in Economics and Media Studies from Mount Holyoke College. Since getting those, she's been busy: she is a professor in, and the head of, the Department of Communication at the University of Illinois, Chicago, the author or editor of three books, most recently *A Private Sphere* (Polity, 2010) and *A Networked Self* (Routledge, 2010), and countless articles and book chapters, and a frequent speaker and lecturer on issues of connectivity and community, as well as public and private concerns.

ROY CHRISTOPHER: *If you had to sum it up for the uninitiated, what would you say your work is about? What are your major areas of concern?*

ZIZI PAPACHARISSI: I am interested in social and political things people do online and offline. I see little value in drawing a distinction between offline and online that treats the two as separate worlds and thus claims some of these interactions as real and others as virtual. To me, that is like suggesting that a phone conversation with someone is less real because it becomes possible through the use of a medium. And many media historians have of course talked about how early reactions to the telephone prompted similar conversations about the complexion and reality of mediated conversations.

I do think it is meaningful, however, to think of offline and online spaces and understand then how people traverse through these spaces in their everyday routines. People adjust and adopt their behaviors as they move from one space to another, so as to handle their interactions in a way that permits them to attain an optimal balance = happiness. Spaces draw out different aspects of our personalities and inspire us to do different things<— or might leave us completely uninspired. We also frequently design or reorganize spaces so as to suit our personalities. There are particular types of behaviors that work better or facilitate communication in certain spaces (for example, speaking loudly in crowded bars), but are utterly discouraged via the organizational logic of other spaces (for example, yelling in a yoga class). I am very interested in how individuals develop behaviors that allow them to traverse through offline and online spaces fluently.

I do not find the term "social media" particularly useful. All media are social, in their own unique ways. To claim that some media are social implies that there are other media that are a-social, or anti-social. It also suggests social media are more social than other media not qualified by that label. I do not find that to be the case. The phrase also ascribes a certain neutrality to the term medium, and I do not believe in that either<— media are neither good, nor bad, nor are they neutral, à la Melvin Kranzberg. I prefer to think of technology as architecture, in case that was not abundantly clear already.

RC: *danah boyd's equation for privacy entails context and control.*

With the convergence of technology and its blurring of boundaries you discuss in A Private Sphere *(Polity, 2010) — especially those that define space and time, public and private, active and passive, producer and consumer — how are we to maintain control of these shifting contexts?*

ZP: I agree with danah and find that this is a tremendously meaningful way of explaining privacy to the public and to policy-making communities. I have a slight preference for the term autonomy over that of control. Perhaps it is because I am Greek. In *A Private Sphere* I use Deleuze's work to explain how control is ultimately not about discipline. So, control, from the perspective of the individual or from the perspective of society or institutions, is about offering a number of possibilities so that people can choose "freely," while not being restricted yet still perfectly guided by a defined set of possibilities. Autonomy is about having the right to determine what those possibilities will be, to choose from them, or to refuse them altogether. Autonomy also is suggestive of self-reliance, independence, self-governance, and reflexivity of the self, or individuation.

I suppose I find that ultimately, life is about philosophizing your way out of the concept of control to a state of autonomy, and that might be why I am partial to the latter word. But in the end, you know, it is just a word. A definition.

RC: *The web and mobile devices have changed the ways we connect with each other, but has social media really changed the nature of those connections?*

ZP: The youth has always redefined things, and I hope they never stop. It is what they do best! Otherwise, what is the point of being young?

On the topic of "friendship," the literature shows that people handle their friendships in different ways across different spaces, and that has always been the case. We have always had friends from a number of social spheres (for example, work, college, childhood, through mutual/spousal/familial acquaintances), sometimes these spheres overlap and sometimes they do not, and we socialize with friends on a number of spaces, including spaces facilitated by internet platforms. Friendship means different things to different people. We also adjust and evolve our perspective on friendships as we mature through the different cycles of our lives. So everything that "the youth" is doing on Facebook needs to be understood in this context.

So, if anything, we might say that the word is being redefined, not the actual meaning of friendship, or its closeness. It is a matter of language evolving so as to reflect our practices. Weak ties can be actually be very strong, but is that really a term to be used to describe anyone? Who wants to be told, "I do not consider you a friend, but you sure are a meaningful weak tie to me," or "btw, I also consider you an important acquaintance." So, as a society, we must come up with words that value and provide social context for these connections that may now be maintained and activated in more convenient ways.

Friendship is an abstraction, a word invented to refer to and measure other emotions that are also aggregates and temporally sensitive. But friendship, or whatever it might be called in the future, is not going anywhere. It has always been a survival strategy for social beings and will always be.

RC: *Along the same lines, I've been thinking a lot about the way that the adoption, or lack thereof, of communication technology in general changes the idea of communication — what I've been calling the "tyranny of adoption." For instance, the diffusion of the cellphone has made it a personal assumption, a requirement in many cases, and one can see this with social networking sites and lifestreaming media as well. How do we temper the spread of technology with our personal needs and desires?*

ZP: I think we need to find a place for technology in our lives. In that sense, we blend technology with our own humanity and resist or challenge the tyranny of adoption. In our everyday lives, we routinely make decisions about what works or what does not. So, we do not choose to buy and use just any car, we buy the car that will fit our needs, our budget, our personality. We also choose to not buy a car and rely on public transport. We choose clothing, houses, appliances that are compatible with our lifestyles and enhance our lives. We may not always make successful or optimal choices, but we are driven by the need to select. At the same time, our choices are shaped by the options we have at hand. And our socio-cultural context may present some of these options as more appealing or popular than others.

I am not sure that we will ever be able to fully escape the tyranny of the popular, or of adoption. Afterall, the capitalist backbone of our economic system rewards the popular. But I think of it less as a tyranny and more of as a habitus. Ultimately, they may both be understood as systems of control, but I suppose a habitus also embeds the notion of reflexivity, socio-cultural context, taste — it is a richer way to think about this. So, in a sense, we might think of not the tyranny of, let's say, Facebook adoption but rather, the Facebook habitus, as a way of socializing us into and remediating schemata, tastes, and habits about friendship.

RC: *Are you working on anything, have anything coming up, or just a topic I missed that you'd like to mention here?*

ZP: A lot of people these days are interested in the notion of affect, or jouissance, and affective networks. I think there is a lot of potential in thinking about affect, as it permits us to understand content creation as both play and work; to look at the internet, in Trebor Scholz's terms, as both playground and factory. Lately I have been very interested in the performative aspect of play online, specifically as it applies to performances of the self in everyday life. So I have been reading a lot of performance theory and working with the "as-if" aspect of play to understand how people imagine, perform, then redact and remix identities online.

11

DOUGLAS RUSHKOFF
The User's Dilemma

Interview by Roy Christopher
Illustration by Laura Persat
October 8, 2010

For over two decades, Douglas Rushkoff has been dragging us all out near the horizon, trying to show us glimpses of our own future. Though he's written books on everything from counterculture and video games to advertising and Judaism, he's always maintained a media theorist's bent: one part Marshall McLuhan, one part Neil Postman, and one part a mix of many significant others. *Program or Be Programmed: Ten Commands for a Digital Age* (O/R Books, 2010) finds him back at the core of what he does. Simply put, this little book, running just shy of 150 pages, is the missing manual for our wild, wired world.

Rushkoff agrees with many media thinkers that we are going through a major shift in the way we conceive, connect, and communicate with each other. His concern is that we're conceding control of this shift to forces that may not have our best interests in mind. "We teach kids how to use software to write," he writes, "but not how to write software. This means they have access to the capabilities given to them by others but not the power to determine the value-creating capabilities of these technologies for themselves." We're conceiving our worlds using metaphors invented by others. This is an important insight and one that helps make up the core of his critique. This book is more Innis's biases of media than it is McLuhan's laws of media, and it left me astounded, especially after reading several books on the subject that were the textual equivalent of fly-over states. *Program or Be Programmed* is a welcome stop along the way.

ROY CHRISTOPHER: Program or Be Programmed *seems to distill quite a lot of your thinking about our online world from the past twenty-odd years. What prompted you to directly address these issues now?*

DOUGLAS RUSHKOFF: I guess it's because the first generation of true "screenagers" or digital natives have finally come of age and, to my surprise, seem less digitally literate than their digital immigrant counterparts. I've written a number of books applying the insights of digital culture — of its DIY, hacker ethos — to other areas, such as government, religion, and the economy. But I realize that we don't even relate to digital culture from the perspective of cultural programmers. We tend to accept the programs we use as given circumstances rather than as the creations of people with intentions.

So, I wanted to go back and write something of a "poetics" of digital media, sharing the main biases of digital technologies so that people can approach them as real users, makers, and programmers rather than just as passive consumers.

If anything in particular prompted me, it was watching the way smart writers and thinkers were arguing back and forth in books and documentaries about whether digital technology is good for us or bad for us. I think it's less a question of what the technology is doing to us than what we are choosing to do to one another with these technologies. If we're even choosing anything at all.

RC: *You mention in the book that anyone who seems a bit too critical of digital media is labeled a Luddite and a party-pooper,* *yet you were able to be critical, serious, and hopeful all at the same time. What's the difference between your approach and that of other critics of all-things-digital?*

DR: I think the main difference is that I'm more concerned with human intention and how it is either supported or repressed in the digital realm. Empathy is repressed, the ability to connect over long distances is enhanced. I go down to the very structure and functioning of these tools and interfaces to reveal how they are intrinsically biased toward certain kinds of outcomes.

So, I'm less concerned with how a technology affects us than how our application or misapplication of a technology works for or against our intentions. And, perhaps more importantly, how the intentions of our programmers remain embedded in the technologies we use. I'm not judging a technology one way or the other; rather, I am calling for people to make some effort to understand what the technologies they are using were made for and whether that makes it the right tool for the job they're using it for.

RC: *You evoke Harold Innis throughout this book. Do you think there's something that he covers more thoroughly or usefully than other media theorists since?*

DR: I think he was better at looking at media shaping the nature and tenor of the social activity occurring on it or around it. He's the guy who would have seen how cell phones change the nature of our social contract on the street, turning a once-public space into lots of separate, little, private spaces. As far as media-ecology goes, he was probably the purest theorist.

RC: *The last programming class I took was a Visual Basic class in which even the programming was obscured by a graphical interface: there was little in the way of real code. For those of us interested, what's the first step in becoming a programmer now?*

DR: I guess it depends on your interests. There are many different places to start. You could go back and learn Basic, one of the simplest computer languages, in order to see the way lines of code in a program flow. Or you could even just get a program like Director and sequence some events. Hypercard was a great little tool that gave people a sense of running a script.

If I were starting, I'd just grab a big, fat book that starts from the beginning, like Dan Shiffman's book *Learning Processing* (Morgan Kaufman, 2008). You can sit down with a book like that and, with no knowledge at all, end up with a fairly good sense of programming in a couple of weeks.

I'm not asking everyone be a programmer at this point. Not this generation, anyway. That's a bit like asking illiterate adults to learn how to read when they can just listen the radio or books on tape. I get that. But for those who will be living in increasingly digital spaces, programming will amount to the new literacy.

RC: *Though you never stray too far, you seem to have come back to your core work in this book. What's next?*

DR: I have no idea, really. Having come "home" to a book on pure media theory applied to our real experience, I feel like I've returned to my core competence. I feel like I should stick here a while and talk about these issues for a year or so until they really sink in.

I've got a graphic novel coming out next year, finally, called *ADD*. It's about kids who are raised from birth (actually, earlier) to be video game testers. I'd love to see that story get developed for other media and then get to play around in television or film. There are also rumblings about doing another *Frontline* documentary. Something following up on "Digital Nation," which I'd like to do in order to get more of my own ideas out there to the non-reading public.

I guess we'll see.

12

danah boyd
Privacy = Context + Control

Interview by Roy Christopher
Illustration by Laura Persat
September 11, 2010

danah boyd is one of the very few people worthy of the oft-bandied title "social media expert" and the only one who studies social technology use with as much combined academic rigor and popular appeal. She holds a PhD from University of California, Berkeley's iSchool and is currently a Senior Social Media Researcher at Microsoft Research New England and a Fellow at Harvard University's Berkman Center for Internet and Society. As the debates over sharing, privacy, and the online control of both smolder in posts and articles web-wide, boyd remains one of a handful of trustworthy, sober voices.

boyd's thoughts on technology and society are widely available online, as well as in the extensive essay collection, *Hanging Out, Messing Around, and Geeking Out* (MIT Press, 2009). In what follows, we discuss several emerging issues in social media studies, mostly online privacy, which has always been a concern as youth and digital media become ever more intertwined.

ROY CHRISTOPHER: *Facebook is catching a lot of flak lately regarding their wishy-washy Terms of Service and their treatment* *of their members' privacy. Is there something happening that's specific to Facebook, or is it a coincidental critical mass of awareness of online privacy issues?*

DANAH BOYD: Facebook plays a central role in the lives of many people. People care about privacy in that they care about understanding a social situation and wisely determining what to share in that context and how much control they have over what they share. This is not to say that they don't also want to be public; they do. It's just that they also want control. Many flocked to Facebook because it allowed them to gather with friends and family and have a semi-private social space. Over time, things changed. Facebook's recent changes have left people confused and frustrated, lacking trust in the company and wanting a space where they can really connect with the people they care about without risking social exposure. Meanwhile, many have been declaring privacy dead. Yet, that's not the reality for everyday folks.

RC: *Coincidentally, I just saw yours and Samantha Biegler's report on risky online behavior and young people. The news loves a juicy online scandal, but their worries always seem so overblown to those in-the-know. What should we do about it?*

DB: Find a different business model for news so that journalists don't resort to sensationalism? More seriously, I don't know how to combat a lot of fear mongering. It's not just journalists. It's parents and policy makers and educators. People are afraid, and they fear what they don't know. It's really hard to grapple with that. But what really bothers me about the fear mongering is that it obscures the real risks that youth face while also failing to actually help the youth who are most at-risk.

RC: *New York University's Jay Rosen maintains that in his Twitter feed, he tries to be "100 percent personal and zero percent private." Is that just fancy semantics or is there something more to that?*

DB: The word "private" means many things. There are things that Jay keeps private. For example, I've never seen a sex tape produced by Jay. I've never read all of his emails. I'm not saying that I want to but just that living in public is not a binary. Intimacy with others is about protecting a space for privacy between you and that other person. And I don't just mean sexual intimacy. My best friend and I have conversations to which no one else is privy, not because they're highly secretive but because we expose raw emotional issues to one another that we're not comfortable sharing with everyone. Hell, we're often not sure that we're comfortable admitting our own feelings to ourselves. That's privacy. And when I post something online that's an injoke to some people but perfectly visible to anyone, that's privacy. And when I write something behind a technical lock like email or a friends-only account because I want to minimize how far it spreads, that's privacy. But in that case, I'm relying more on the individuals with whom I'm sharing than the technology itself. Privacy isn't a binary that can be turned on or off. It's about context, social situations, and control.

RC: *Hannah Arendt defines the private and public realms respectively as "the distinction between things that should be hidden and things that should be shown." How do you define the distinction?*

DB: I would say the public is where we go to see and be seen while minimizing our vulnerabilities while the private is where we expose ourselves in a trusted space with trusted individuals.

13

Dave Allen
Every Force Evolves a Form

Interview by Roy Christopher
Illustration by Laura Persat
May 7, 2008

I can't remember the first time I heard Gang of Four, but I do distinctly remember a lot of things making sense once I did. Their jagged and angular bursts of guitar, funky rhythms, deadpan vocals, and overtly personal-as-political lyrics predated so many other bands I'd been listening to. Dave Allen was the man behind the bass, and now he's the man behind *Pampelmoose*, a Portland-based, music and media blog.

I sat down with Dave last summer for a lengthy shop-talk session over Mexican food, and I managed to glean the following dialogue from it. We talked about Gang of Four, Dave's personal history from forming that band to running *Pampelmoose*, the questionable state of the music industry, and why Portland is the place to be.

An update was planned, but now that Dave, along with drummer Hugo Burnham, has parted ways with Gang of Four again, I figured I'd go ahead and run this interview as-is. Dave's ideas about the state of the record industry, about which he's written extensively on *Pampelmoose*, and how Gang of Four should release their music clash with the band's more traditional leanings. The seeds of his departure can be seen germinating in the talk below.

ROY CHRISTOPHER: *Seeing all of the sound-alike bands around, you guys originally got back together and did your old material.*

DAVE ALLEN: Yeah, the point that that was really validated was when we played in the West of England at the All Tomorrow's Parties "Nightmare Before Christmas" show, curated by Thurston Moore, and we were the co-headliners. We'd already played with them the previous summer at the Prima Vera festival in Barcelona. We actually followed them that night, and I was really concerned, but what I realized was, although that band puts out new albums every now and again — *Sonic Nurse* and *Rather Ripped* — they make great records. They never stopped. Now, you might argue that nothing changes with Sonic Youth, so their style is the same: you just get a new batch of songs from Sonic Youth. And there's something remarkably comforting about that, but, at the same time, the moment when they launch into something from *Daydream Nation,* they expand on it because they're a jam-band at times, but the most interesting jam-band ever to be seen live. They are such a superb band. Forget everyone else. But it dawned on me, we and they are legacy bands. People don't necessarily come to hear the new material. So, you better be sure to pack your set with a lot of old material. They've got twenty albums to draw on, right? We've only got two. Really. It limits the amount of time we can be on stage, but, at the same time, we're not ones to overstay our welcome. Live, those songs are more intense than ever before. They have a new vibe that I really like.

Anyway, point being, once you realize that people are coming to see you to hear the old songs, including the new crowd that turns up, by the way, then you're okay.

If we do record twelve new songs, six of which are really good, then how do we put that out? My argument would be that we're Gang of Four, and we're supposed to do things a bit differently. So, do we do it through a cell-phone provider? Something different. Or should we give it away digitally and just press some heavy-gram vinyl to sell at shows? The days of doing a CD are over. That's my argument. Now, I don't know if Jon and Andy would agree, but the point being is that the material can be used in many different ways. There's one idea that we've been kicking around with this new song that I really like. Jon's got this thing about caffeine culture, and it's a really cool direction we're going in, and it's good, old-fashioned Gang of Four. I'm really enjoying it. Now, what if we perversely actually went to Red Bull or whoever and see if they want to release it? It's not available anywhere else except in their ad. Then make it viral online where you can download the Red Bull/Gang of Four video, and so on. That way it gets spread around the globe in different ways. And the point being is not to sell anything, but Red Bull would pay us for the campaign, and we get back on the road, which is where we do best. We play live, we get paid well, we can sell t-shirts and vinyl, so the concept of signing to a label, putting something out, and touring on it is so ridiculous to me. If we don't own the idea, there's no point in doing it.

RC: *Right, it's just like the legacy idea. You've used the Rolling Stones as an example. The new records are just an excuse to get out on the road and play the old songs live.*

DA: That's all it is.

RC: *Do they really realize that? You say they do, but I think it's that you realize that. I don't think the Rolling Stones think of themselves as a legacy band. I think they're still trying to make another "great" Rolling Stones record.*

DA: I think you're right. That's the counterpoint, right? They may not have realized it and I think all bands want to keep creating, and what I'm saying is —

RC: *"We've done our good stuff. Let's just keep doing it."*

DA: Right. There are other ways to be creative, so I would argue that doing my label and trying to find new bands is creative, and now I've got my heavily trafficked blog.

RC: *Right. You have an outlet, and you get to play live.*

DA: Yeah, why would we kill ourselves to do a new record when no one wants to buy it anyway?

RC: *There's no good way to say it.*

DA: It's all downhill. It's retreat.

RC: *Yeah, when you first mentioned the legacy band idea, it really resonated with me, but I finally got around to watching the Metallica documentary,* Some Kind of Monster, *and wow. Those guys are just so obviously past their prime and just killing themselves trying to make a new record. It just ends up being a parody of what they once were, and I think that really speaks to your idea of being a legacy band — and realizing it.*

DA: I would argue that who's to blame here are the labels. The labels are to blame. It's like when Coldplay decided not to make an album because Apple was about to be born, and Chris couldn't write songs or whatever, EMI's shares dropped 15 percent, because it was all about the biggest band on the label. Well, Metallica are huge, so it's the same thing. All the heads of Warner Brothers will be pushing them, "look at the share price! We need an album from you guys!"

RC: *It was totally like that in the film! When James left for rehab, the label freaked, like "oh my god, our cash cow is falling apart!"*

DA: Well, didn't Geffen pretty much go away after Kurt killed himself? Nirvana was Geffen's cash cow.

RC: *Not like they lost any when he died... In 1995, Sub-Pop's second biggest seller was Sebadoh's Bakesale. Their first? Nirvana's* Bleach! *In 1995, Sub-Pop could have not released anything and just kept* Bleach *on the market, and they would've still made money.*

DA: So, my point about these legacy bands making records is, the Rolling Stones will be given a million dollars every time they want to make a record. The label can recoup that money. They're not going to get rich off of the record, but it revitalizes the back catalog and puts the band on the road. Otherwise, why would they bother to get out of bed to record? They're past their prime as songwriters. I'm sorry, there's not anything redeeming about it.

I think it's interesting that Sting got The Police back together but didn't bother to make a record with those guys. And Sting is the consummate songwriter. Meanwhile, the cheapest ticket on the Police tour is a hundred dollars.

RC: *You know how much the good ones are? Nine-hundred.*

DA: Are they?! Let's go back to that one-hundred dollars: there goes the music industry! The live side of it is growing, but there goes the recording industry. The back catalog is the only money to be made.

RC: *What about Mötley Crüe? They had to prop Mick Marrs up, and Vince Neil is huffing and puffing and barely making it through one of those tours. They made millions of dollars and didn't even do a new record!*

DA: You don't need to.

RC: *Kiss did, what, three reunion tours? And all three of those years, those were the biggest tours of the year.*

DA: People don't want to hear the new material.

RC: *They want to hear "Rock and Roll All Nite."*

DA: It's a reminder of your youth.

RC: *It's nostalgia marketing.*

DA: Absolutely.

RC: *It's one of the strongest things out there.*

DA: It's what we did on our holidays, twenty years ago.

RC: *Right.*

—

RC: *So, why Portland?*

DA: In late 1999, I was living in Lookout Mountain with my kids, all computer kids, and I went to a friend of mine, Nigel Phelps, who's one of the top art directors in the movies — he did Titanic and all sorts of big movies, English guy. His eldest daughter, I saw that she was on the computer, on AOL, and she was talking to herself saying, "you're on dial-up, you're not on broadband," and I asked her if she was arguing with someone about who was on dial-up and who was on broadband. She said, "no." On Napster, when you selected a song it tells you the bandwidth availability. So, when it was really slow, she would IM the person and say, "you liar. You're on a 28K dial-up. You're not on broadband." That was my first exposure to Napster, and I was like, "what the heck is this?" I look and she's got all of this free music. Now, I was at eMusic, where we charged 99 cents per song, and, the next morning, I went into the office and emailed the head guys and said, "guys, you're done. Everybody is getting free music from Napster." Their attitude was that it was illegal and that they'd soon be put out of business. And I was saying, "not before we go out of business." And that's exactly what happened.

Then, around 2000, when the market sank and the whole dotcom thing fell in the toilet, I got the call that they were closing the Los Angeles office. I got a call from a headhunter that some guys in Portland wanted to fly me up and talk to me and would like to hire me for a similar position. I liked Portland, I'd been here a lot, I had friends here already, but I wasn't ready to leave the big city just yet. Anyway, it turned out to be Intel, and, on the campus here right outside Portland, they had this thing called New Business Investments, or NBI, and I was asked to join the Consumer Digital Audio Services, or something like that. It sounded interesting, so I joined up. They were looking at internet-connected devices, an MP3 player — pre-iPod — and different ways to get your music and Home Entertainment servers. And the thing we were building, that you see now, was this bridging system that transmitted music files from your computer to your legacy Hi-Fi. 802.11b had just arrived, so we were working to get the music from there to there, wirelessly. My job was to go to Yahoo music and other content providers and license them for our service. It was a great idea. The problem was, Intel is known for developing amazing stuff and then getting cold feet at the last minute and not bringing it to market. At home I've got five MP3 players that are better than the iPod. There's a soundcard in them, engineered to perfection. They're amazing. The only problem was that it's just a flash device, it only had a 128Kb flash card for memory, and no one had thought of an adding slot where you could upgrade the memory. Never came to market. That was that.

They'd paid for me and my family to move up, I'd bought a great house, and I think it's a great city. I don't feel the urge to move back. I'm a booster for this town. I love it.

RC: *I've only been here for two months, but every other day there's someone else here that I didn't know was here, or some event that I didn't realize happened here. I never thought about moving here because Seattle has been my adopted home for so many years, so I never thought about dropping down here. But since I did, it's an amazing town.*

DA: Anthony Keidis just moved here.

RC: *Really?*

DA: Ironic, huh? Now I can ask him about my royalties. [Laughs] "You can come to my barbecue. Please bring blank check." [Laughs] Everyone's here. The Shins, Johnny Marr…

RC: *His being in Modest Mouse…*

DA: You can say it, Roy.

RC: *Okay, I hate Modest Mouse. [Laughs] I love Johnny Marr, but I hate Modest Mouse. It's funny that the Mouse House is right over there.*

DA: Yeah, I ran into Isaac Brock's girlfriend, and he came by the office to get some stuff, and he said I should come over, that there's someone there I'd probably like to meet. So, I went over there, and I walk upstairs and there's Johnny Marr. He sees me walk in and he's like, "what the fucking hell are you doing in Portland?" And I said, "well, what the fucking hell are you doing in Portland?" [Laughs]

They're an interesting band to watch because they were a multi-platinum band, and now they're not. You have to make money on the road.

RC: *That's another area that hip-hop is missing out on. Hip-hop is not known for big live shows — and it should be. The lyrical element of hip-hop is one of the most exciting things to see live, but the acts that excel at that part of it are not the acts that are selling the records and doing those tours.*

DA: The underground aspect is interesting, like, The Roots do well touring, Blackalicious… But the bigger it gets, the more it slows down. I mean, is T.I. going to do a big arena tour?

RC: *No, but T.I. is one of the guys who's still selling records.*

DA: Yeah, he's fine, but the minute it drops off, what can he fall back on?

RC: *Right. Then he can go be Jay-Z.*

DA: That may be one of the things that hurt live hip-hop: it was so easy to sell records, it was like why bother going on the road?

RC: *Well, for a long time hip-hop had a hard time getting security for shows because it had been tainted with this "violence" tag.*

DA: And it was never as bad really as your average big rock show. It's just racism.

RC: *Yeah, it's a race thing and something the press loves to play up, and it's completely untrue, but it keeps you from getting insurance for a hip-hop show. The reality is, the insurance company is like, "Ice Cube? Oh, hell no!"*

DA: Right. Every Black person is packing, and there are 50,000 of them in an arena, we're not covering that. And then Guns N' Roses comes to town and there are two stabbing deaths —

RC: *And all of the seats in the arena are ripped out and thrown on stage.*

DA: Yeah, but those are all white guys from the suburbs.

—

RC: *So, what are your goals with* Pampelmoose?

DA: It started it off like it did with my label World Domination, maybe a little too starry-eyed. I feel I've done really well in music, and I'm generally a very positive person.

RC: *That's one of the things I love about you, Dave.*

DA: Aw, thanks. [Laughs] I look at bands and at the scene, and I feel like I've got to give back. I volunteer a lot and I try and help, probably to my detriment, too much sometimes. So, I worry that I start off with great ambitions and sometimes let people down, because you get over-burdened and everybody wants a piece of it. You back up and think, "I can't do everyone, so I shouldn't do anyone."

RC: *It's hard to find a balance there.*

DA: It is. It's so difficult, but I think we've found some kind of balance with Pampelmoose, and a group of friends and I were able to apply ourselves to a website that became a company that can help artists to sell some of their stuff, come on by anytime for free advice, bring their contracts. I have a lawyer friend who charges very little to look over that stuff. *Pampelmoose* is also an extension of my social life. I'm very active socially. I can't be at home. I've got to be out. I like being with people, and that's no offense to my family. I like being with them, too. So, Pampelmoose has become an extension of my personality. I've tried things like this in the past with fanzines and writing, but it's so difficult. You have to get them printed, get them out there.

RC: *It wasn't a fanzine, Dave. It was an art project. [Laughs]*

DA: That's true, and that's my problem too, I get too deep into the project, and it gets too ambitious and takes on a life of its own, then after the fall, I realize I over did it again. With *Pampelmoose,* the safety net was the blog. Because once the blog took off — and I believe it was January 2006 was the first post — I had no idea where it was going to go, but I did have the idea that I could open the doors to a community. That's the thing I love about blogging, with the comments, people can call bullshit on me. The interesting thing for me was that six months went by, and no one's calling bullshit, and then you get confident. And it wasn't a lot at first, I think in the early days if we got a thousand visitors in a month, that was a lot. But it did pick up and start attracting visitors. Then I began to take it as seriously as everything else I was doing. I'm the editor. I'm the public voice. I'm the journalist. I'm the copy editor. I'm the layout guy. And at first, I thought I might be building something that I couldn't maintain, so I hired a bit of a support team. Then I learned to fly. I learned some basic HTML code, I learned to crop photos. Every post has an image, any image. It doesn't have to go with the rest of the story. So, it has a little art aspect to it, if you will. In the past eighteen months it's morphed totally into this blog. Pampelmoose is the blog, and, as a side note, we still sell CDs, T-shirts, and give advice to local bands. So, getting up every day and having an opinion and having people comment on it drives the whole thing, and now that the traffic is up, it's like, "oh, shit."

RC: *Yeah, but it validates everything you're doing there.*

DA: Right, but just having explained it, it's still weird. It's not like we're Wal-Mart, and we do this.

RC: *Right, but with Wal-Mart, there's a precedent. "Remember K-Mart? Like that, but better." When you're doing something like this, it's more ambiguous. People ask me what my book is about, and I say it's a collection of interviews. "Well, what's the theme?" You have to read it. So, it's frustrating, but if you read it, you get it. Even if you only read one interview per section, a theme emerges. I think Pampelmoose is the same way. If you go there and dig around, read, and become a part of it, it fits, but there's no one-line explanation for what's going on there.*

DA: It is intriguing. It's not *Pitchfork*, where they get a million hits a month, and it's like, "what's the point?" At the same time, I can't deny their success. They've done it well, but now you've got this unfettered fan-boy day out where you can kill something before it even has a chance.

HIP-HOP

14

JUICE ALEEM
Don't Be Afraid of the Dark

Interview by Roy Christopher
Illustration by Eleanor Purcell
July 23, 2018

Once a member of the brain-forward UK crew New Flesh for Old, Juice Aleem has long since stepped out on his own. Griff Rollefson writes in his book *Flip the Script* that on Juice's first solo record, *Jerusalaam Come* (Big Dada, 2009), Aleem "recuperates universalism by locating and privileging a pre-Enlightenment performative linguistics." In other words, he uses his lyrics to go back in time in order to envision a better future. His latest record, *Voodu StarChild* (Gamma Proforma, 2017), continues his quest to create not just better visions of the future but also better futures for real.

Friend and fellow emcee Mike Ladd tells me,

> I first met Juice when on the Infesticons tour in the UK in 2001, I think. We didn't have enough money to bring over the whole band so Juice filled in. Rob Sonic and I were so drunk every show that Juice did all the rapping. Mostly freestyle, I think. Since then, Juice has been a consummate collaborator and best friend. I know few emcees personally who are as introspective thoughtful and as studious as Juice. This man has

volumes of knowledge at his disposal and dispenses them with a gentlemanly generosity... Juice will blow your mind on stage as a performer and off stage as a friend. Every time. Without fail.

I've been in touch Juice for the past few years, and I concur with Mike Ladd: he has always been genuine, generous, and supportive. Juice's old crew, New Flesh, did some tracks and shows with the god Rammellzee back in the early aughts, so I had to ask him a bit about that as well.

ROY CHRISTOPHER: *Your first solo record,* Jerusalaam Come, *goes back to a precolonial time in order to imagine a better future. Is there an underlying aim with* Voodu StarChild? *If so, what's the story?*

JUICE ALEEM: Yeah, there are several themes and aims within *Voodu StarChild*. A lot of it is about people being aware of the magic inside themselves and understanding how that is under attack. How that hidden self is dark, female energy, and it's questioned at every moment. Our original selves are out of equilibrium in regard the male and female balance, and this album is a play on that. It's not only a critique, but it has a few answers within on how I address certain parts of this for myself and those around me in regard to things like diet, family, love, and when to go to war.

For years we have been taught that Voodu is a bad thing, when it is our own personal rituals and practices that will do a better job of saving us than the politicians and the religious have done so far. There is nothing to fear in the dark.

RC: *In your book* Afrofutures and Astro Black Travel: A Passport to Melanated Futures *(Malik Books, 2016), you talk about hackers and whistleblowers. What do you see as the connections between them and hip-hop?*

JA: To me there are many connections between them all. The hacker is the most obvious though with the wiretap on all the juicy insides of whatever tech is already out there. Using everything from drum pads and samplers to magpie the last few centuries of speeches, music, and commercials and turn them upside-in for the betterment of the practitioner and listener. Hip-hop is hacking.

The whistleblower is also well seen in hip-hop form, from P.E. telling us "Don't Believe the Hype" to Kanye telling us "George Bush doesn't care about Black people." The moments are loads with little between. Hip-hop traditionally has been one of the biggest whistleblowers out there till recent years. I'm sure the new gen can get there too in between the adverts for big pharma opiates.

RC: *You've been organizing and hosting festivals and workshops and such. Tell me about those.*

JA: Workshops have been a thing on and off since Lord Redeem started the Ghetto Grammar sessions back in the mid-'90s. I helped out, then he and myself took it London and UK wide. Since then, I've worked and tutored in many places including schools, youth centers, universities, and even a few prisons. Even got caught up doing work in France in a prison outside of Paris.

It's not something I do every day, but I like to bring it back now and then for certain projects such as my lyric-writing workshop as part of this year's AfroFlux events within the B-SIDE Hip-Hop Festival here in Birmingham, UK. B-SIDE has been running three years now, and this year had around ten-thousand visitors over the weekend in May.

I'm one of the core, artistic directors of B-SIDE and the main person behind AfroFlux: it's a concept where we look to celebrate the Black and Brown thinkers and makers who don't usually get the accolades while also applying hands on practical applications of cultural markers such as Afrofuturism. We have had a few stand-alone events and plan to expand on that with our partners in other parts of the globe.

RC: *You and I were talking before about Rammellzee. Did his work influence your own?*

JA: In a way, but similar to others' in his kind of cultural echelon, you don't always realize 'til looking back, and also seeing that part of the reason you like them and their art so much is due to the parts of self that have a resonance within the artist you look at. Ramm is a perfect mirror for the things you'd never think would be reflected and magnified. There are things I had thought before I ever knew of Ramm, and to see a person not only having a knowledge of things but living them to the full is his real influence on me. Not just on my art but the living of it, being all aspects of my thoughts and creations.

RC: *You recorded a song with him with your old crew New Flesh for Old. What can you tell me about that session?*

JA: We did a few songs, two of which made it to the *Understanding* (Big Dada, 2002) album. They were a little out there, 'cause those were the days of still recording songs in the same studio with people actually being there. So, having these songs come from Ramm rambling down the phone at all hours and of us making sense of it was a real new thing. Then he sent tapes over to Part 2, and we edited the pieces we liked best. There was intended to be a whole series of stories from his cosmic opera. "Mack Facts" was cool 'cause we had a theme of this whole future arena style thing with us being the gladiators and Ramm as the announcer. Think of an intense episode of that Gwar, *Mad Max* show starring Sonny Chiba and Sho Kosugi as Nuba warriors on Plutonia. Speaking with him and listening to him so much on those tapes was kinda trippy, and how he'd take any little idea and run with it creating a session's worth of vocals. This wasn't your average 16 bars but reams and reams of classic adventure rasped in an intense style that fully drew you in. We still have a few bits and pieces from those sessions.

RC: *What's coming up?*

JA: As per usual there are a lot of things happening. My three main things I'm gearing up for right now are a new festival in Birmingham by the name of High Vis Festival. It's a bunch of art-loving heads such as myself and graffiti writers like Mose, Panda, and Wingy who have decided to put on a festival highlighting comics, street art, graffiti, zine culture, and other visual movements with a strong ethic in serious street culture.

A couple of gigs with the Exile All Stars, which is myself, Mike Ladd, and TIE. We have all been friends for a while and have promised to take new music and perform it. This is the promise.

The number three is from even longer ago, and it's all about new music from Shadowless. We took the passing of one our brothers by the name of Defisis to cement the call for new tunes. Watch this space.

RC: *Is there anything else you'd like to throw in?*

JA: Do not be afraid of your own Voodu.

15

LABTEKWON
Margin Walker

Interview by Roy Christopher
Illustration by Josh Row
July 12, 2017

Baltimore emcee Labtekwon has been described as "the Thelonius Monk of hip-hop" by Chuck D, and a cross between Jean Michel Basquiat and Nikola Tesla by Afropunk. He's outspoken like any good rapper could be, skilled like any good emcee would be, and motivated like any good activist should be. He stays consistently ahead of and outside of the time the rest of us dwell in.

Labtekwon is an anthropologist, a professor, a writer, an emcee, and a skateboarder. As he says, "books and songs are just different rivers and lakes with the same water." His first record came out over two decades ago. This is your official wake-up call.

ROY CHRISTOPHER: *The phrase "heads ain't ready" seems an appropriate descriptor of your art. Given how long you've been at it, do you think they will ever be?*

LABTEKWON: Well, a lot of pop stars bite off of me usually two or three years after I do something, so I think it's more of an issue of mass media exposure, and, at present I think "heads" are "ready" for innovation and mastery. But in terms of American pop culture, historically, the masses have never been connected to great art in real time, due to the nature of capitalism and what Adorno and Horkheimer call "the culture industry." The vanguard of Black art is always detached to the mainstream perception via the entertainment industrial complex, and I understand that my art is a part of that cultural legacy of marginalization.

In terms of the microcosm of interaction with audiences at shows, folks recognize I make a very sophisticated and advanced form of art. Of course if you aren't looking for something you may not know you are "ready" until you experience it. I only have as many listeners as there are people who hear my music.

Ironically, I get direct personal encouragement from conversations with pioneers like Chuck D, Wise Intelligent, and Prince Po. People that really love the art know I am a modern pioneer in the twenty-first century. When emcees and rappers hear me, they know I do difficult and trailblazing things artistically. At the present time though, I am pretty sure if more people knew about my music, I would have many more listeners. I make the art of our times, no retro. Pop culture is just a lagging indicator.

RC: *After the three-part* State of the Art *series and the double-disc* B.O.P., *you took a little longer to release* Sun of Sekhmet. *Was there a reason for the break? Or did you spend that time putting together this record?*

L: Actually, my mother passed away on March 5, 2016 after a struggle with cancer. She started suffering more in late 2015, and I wasn't in a space to make music during that time. I waited until after her funeral to complete the last project. The *Sun of Sekhmet* album was released on her born day of March 16, in 2017 and that was a tribute album to my mother and father. The title reflects the nature of my mother, as Sekhmet is a Kemetic Neter that represents the warrior attribute of the divine feminine Neter, Het Heru. My mother was a Black woman of power, courage, intelligence, purpose, and spirituality, so the double entendre is Sun/Son of Sekhmet.

But I do boxsets and anthologies, the current series is called *The Craft of Imhotep* and the *B.O.P.* album was part one, *Sun of Sekhmet* is part two and the third installment comes out September 21, 2017 and it is called *Khunsu*. So, I am actually releasing two albums in 2017, *Sun of Sekhmet* in the spring and *Khunsu* for autumn. The theme of the current series is each album emphasizes Neter from the Kemetic pantheon:

— *B.O.P.: Tehuti and the Het Heru Cult*
— *Sun of Sekhmet: The Rejected Stone-Mahdi Music*
— *Khunsu*

All of the titles explain the theme of each album, but the series as a whole addresses the demonization of Black Consciousness and a response to the assimilationist agenda.

RC: *You've also written a couple of books.*

L: My master's thesis was a historiographical and anthropological study on the origins of hip-hop culture, and I released it as a book called *The Origins of Hip Hop Culture* in 2014. My first book was essentially the history of the world from 0 CE to 2020 CE in poetry and lyrical form, and that book is called *Labtekwon and The Righteous Indignation,* released in 2012. It is also a music album, but I am a professional anthropologist, historiographer, and professor, so the convergence of my intellectual work is present in my art and vice versa. Books and songs are just different rivers and lakes with the same water.

RC: *Do you still skateboard?*

L: [Laughs.] I can still "ride" a skateboard, but I don't "skate" anymore. Meaning I don't spend eight to twelve hours a day trying to master a trick like I did when I was really skating. I kind of transferred the energy I put into skating into rhyming. I used to split my time between skating and rhyming, but rhyming won.

RC: *What's next on the Labtekwon agenda?*

L: *Khunsu* comes out September 20, 2017, and I have a feature film coming out this year.

16

M. SAYYID
The Other Side

Interview by Roy Christopher
Illustration by Laura Persat
May 17, 2017

Around the bend of the millennium, New York hip-hop collective Antipop Consortium emerged as a voice of possible futures. The spaced-out mix and match of M. Sayyid, Beans, High Priest, and Earl Blaize was a welcome beacon to the hip-hop of the new century. Emcee M. Sayyid's flow is "forward-leaning" and abstract but also as contagious as the flu. He's also the storyteller of the crew, with an unmistakable Slick-Rick-from-the-Dark-Side vibe. Just listen to "9.99" from *Tragic Epilogue* (75 Ark, 2000) or "Z St." from *Arrhythmia* (Warp, 2002).

As with any collection of volatile forces, APC's work as a cohesive group has been sporadic at best, with seven years between their last two, proper full-lengths. As I wrote about the gap in 2009,

> when Antipop Consortium threw down the progressive hip-hop gauntlet on 2002's *Arrhythmia* they didn't expect to have to reunite several years later to pick it up — but they did. Their recent *Fluorescent Black* answers every challenge presented on *Arrhythmia* and then some. It's weird, it's word,

and it's war. The lyrics are abstract but tight, and the beats are quirky but banging — and the whole package will stomp a mudhole in your ass.

Their separate ways are always active in the meantime though, working with everyone from DJ Vadim and DJ Krush to Matthew Shipp and Bill Laswell. As Mike Ladd, who worked with Sayyid on his latest, *Error Tape 1*, tells me,

> like the whole APC crew, always beyond forward. Sayyid is honestly one of my favorite people to work with in music. He always finds a way to push you further constantly challenging himself and those around him in the most positive ways. I've known this brother for almost twenty years and never seen his energy slip. Very, very glad we're in the same town and still get to work together from time to time.

When I first got into APC, I read that M. Sayyid used to work with Mark Pauline's rabid, robot-art crew, Survival Research Laboratories, a fact he confirms below. He also tells me about working with several other familiar, formative names, including Andy Jenkins, Mark Lewman, Spike Jonze, and Nick Philip.

I only recently came across last year's *Error Tape 1* and have had it in rotation nonstop. The "1" in the title ominously hints at future further installments. Sayyid tells me there will be two. "I'm working on tape 2 now," he says.

ROY CHRISTOPHER: *How long have you been in Paris? That has to be mad different from working in New York.*

M. SAYYID: Yeah, I moved here in fall 2013 with my wife who's Parisian. It was super hard to get in the zone, but it had less to do with Paris and more to do with my own personal journey and difficulty finding my sound. Like most things worthwhile, it took time for me to find my sound then it took time for me to understand my vocal character and what my strong points were.

It was about a two-year quest. Once 2015 hit, I had a comfortable studio and engineer vibe.

The biggest achievement was my writing. I had no one around me who could understand what exactly I was saying so it forced me to write from a different place — a place of deep honesty, woven in pattern.

RC: *How did you end up working with Survival Research Laboratories?*

MS: I used to read *RE:Search Magazine* when I moved to San Jose at 18 after high school. I was living in a house of art with Nick Philip and around a lot of Nor-Cal skate culture.

One day I was in a gallery in downtown San Jose, and the owners asked me to help them prepare an exhibition for Mark Pauline. I knew who he was from the magazine, so I was pumped, and I worked that exhibition with him. Also, my homey Chris Cotton was a technician for his Bay Bridge show (insane), so I was around that universe a bunch of times in '89 and '90.

RC: *Did working with SRL inform your music at all?*

MS: For sure, it was the "other side," and I was a magnet for anything on the "other side," and so were the SRL guys. So, when we met, we spoke a similar language.

RC: *Your music always sounds like it's beaming in from some alternate future. What else works its way in there?*

MS: Hmmm… Definitely, my obsession with Basquiat after his death in '89 changed what I thought was possible in the art-making process. I was in an art collective with Andy Jenkins, Spike Jonze, Mark Lewman, and a bunch of other BMX-related folks called The Basement. For literature it was all about Ralph Ellison, Richard Wright, Bukowski. Then musically it was rap, and punk, and people like Laurie Anderson.

Again, all of this was like a way to the "other side."

RC: *What else are you working on that you want to bring up here?*

MS: Promos for *Error Tape 1* (i.e., videos, short tracks, etc.). I provided musical direction and songs for a French-television mini-series that I'm also acting in called Aurore, directed by Laetitia Masson, coming out on Arté.tv in September. I'm also in the process of furthering my creative performance coaching work with a platform for artistic self-improvement called "in-syncro," designed to combine a practice of meditation, physical training, and relaxation for working artists to improve process in art making.

17

SHABAZZ PALACES
A New Refutation

Interview by Roy Christopher
Illustration by Laura Persat
January 25, 2017

The history of hip-hop so far can be seen as split down the middle by the deaths of Biggie Smalls and Tupac Shakur. In the most oversimplified of terms, there was a reset when street sounds gave way to club bangers. Wu-Tang and Nas stepped aside for Missy and Puffy. Few survived.

Ishmael Butler has been on both sides of that divide. His old New York crew, Digable Planets, was all over the place in the early-1990s, and his new Seattle outfit, Shabazz Palaces, is firmly a part of the future, though he doesn't necessarily see time and space like that. Time and space, like reality itself, are human constructs. "Every serious artist hopes not to be a success but to escape the gravity, the pull, the prison of their times," Charles Mudede tells me. "Ish, I think, is the only rapper who achieved escape velocity and is now free in space."

Of the 1993 Digable Planets song "Time & Space (A New Refutation of)," Butler told Brian Coleman in 2007, "that song title was part of the title of the album. It came from Jorge Luis Borges. I was reading a lot of his stuff at the time. ... Everything he wrote was metaphysical and circular, and things didn't always happen for any reason. Time and space are conceptual and can only relate to you as an individual."

After having released one of the most slept-on records in the history of music, 1994's *Blowout Comb* (Pendulum), Digable Planets split up in the mid-1990s. They haven't recorded any new material since, but they've been performing live again since 2005. Don't get it out of sync though, Shabazz Palaces is still Ish's main focus. Their *two* new records, *Quazarz: Born on a Gangster Star* and *Quazarz vs. The Jealous Machines* (both for Sub Pop), come out in July.

ROY CHRISTOPHER: *Now that you've done Digable Planets and Shabazz Palaces simultaneously, how do you approach those two projects differently?*

ISHMAEL BUTLER: I would equate it to how black families have family reunions like every two years. It's like that: getting back to a familiar situation that you don't do that much, but, when you do, it's fun, it's special, and it always reminds you of your home and where you came from. It also makes you think about how you behaved and how you relate to and how you seize the time in the present, you know? So, it's like going back to that music is romantic and nostalgic combined, wrapped up in this present thing that you can touch, but it's still coming from the past, from a past that was very formative. So, it's hard to describe, but I don't think of it like I'm doing them at the same time because I'm really not. The Shabazz thing is now, and Digable shows are shows of older music because we haven't done any new music.

RC: *Would you say that both projects are informed by science fiction?*

IB: Yeah, the first book I ever really read cover to cover was this book called *Z for Zachariah* (Atheneum, 1974). I always liked science fiction movies. I always liked reading science fiction. Octavia Butler came to me in my 20s. I read a lot of that. Then of course there's George Clinton. I don't really call that science fiction, but I call it imaginative reality—where you exist because you believe in different realms, different worlds, natural words, supernatural worlds. You look at a cat like [George] Clinton, and you're like, "oh, he's wild," but he's living in these alternative realities different from ours but no less real. I came onto that early in life.

RC: *The Afrofuturism movement connects the concept of alienation from science fiction with the history of the African diaspora being stolen from their homeland for slavery. Do you think this is a useful connection to make?*

IB: I like the alien aspect of it only because white people were the first to construct this reality that was concrete, had reason, and had form and hierarchies and categories, and you could understand everything, you know? That just wasn't something that African motherfuckers were concerned with. We didn't need to lord over the land and the air and the space and ideas and people—not to that extent. So, when those that did came into contact with us and saw us, that was the birth of science fiction. This notion of a reality, and that we had broken that reality, therefore set into motion all these needs to put hierarchies and to control and to enslave and to have land and borders and all of this kind of stuff. I feel like we are the alien. We deal with this realm in a totally different way than anyone else. And I think that it's shocking and disorienting and calls into question reality. Imagine seeing some niggas in West Africa back then! Who knows what they were capable of doing!

What we did and what we knew and the things we had connections with—it was mind-blowing. It blew people away, and it set into motion all of these things like science fiction and abstraction and cubism and surrealism and all that stuff. I feel like we were catalysts to all of that stuff just by our existence. I look at the Towers in Luxor or the pyramids or different types of structures, and I'm like, yeah, there was some different type of shit going on. I don't think anyone knows what it was, and there are all kinds of theories that are interesting and entertaining and brilliantly conceived, but no one really knows — something else was happening! It appears obvious to me. I hear that when Clinton and those guys get down, when Prince gets down… There's something else at work in these constructions that these people are making.

RC: How do we tell this story right?

IB: If you could somehow get this point across: Every culture — forget race — every culture invented, and was the author of, certain enlightenments and certain constructions. Now, inside of that culture there's skin colors that come from this certain culture. You heard me say I'm not talking about skin: I don't see race like that. White people came up with this code for everything: we got language, we got writing, we got history, which we're going to give an accurate account of, but how! How you gonna give an accurate account of a battle? All these men that died can't read or write, and they're operating at the behest of someone who's in control who's going to author this history! So, forget history altogether! I can't even fuck with it! These are just serial tales that vaguely hint at reality and the truth of some days past, as far as I'm concerned.

I think you've got to figure out how to tell a language-less, history-less story, that is all about expanding the now rather than conquering and controlling the future. That's where all this, quote, "Afrofuturism" comes from is sly motherfuckers who was loving the moment so much that they wanted to blow more air and blow more space into the moment and push it out and hold it as long as they could. That's what grooves and loops and sustaining one groove and one rhythm does: it bends time and melts it and blows bubbles in it. That's what this Afrofuturism stuff is about.

If you came here across the sea in the hull of a ship, and you land, and you start to live this new life in this new territory where it gets extremely cold, and there's all these kinds of seasons and abuse and terrors being pushed upon you. Every minute of every day you live in oppression and terror of the sort that no one can even imagine anymore, no movie can show you anything close to what actually happened. Simple survival, waking up, standing up, greeting the sun, breathing in and out — you're a futurist. You've tapped into something that keeps you moving that's stronger than really anything we've ever seen before from humankind. Imagine getting used to that on a cellular level — you're breathing that now — what's going to be the result of that? I think we all are futurists.

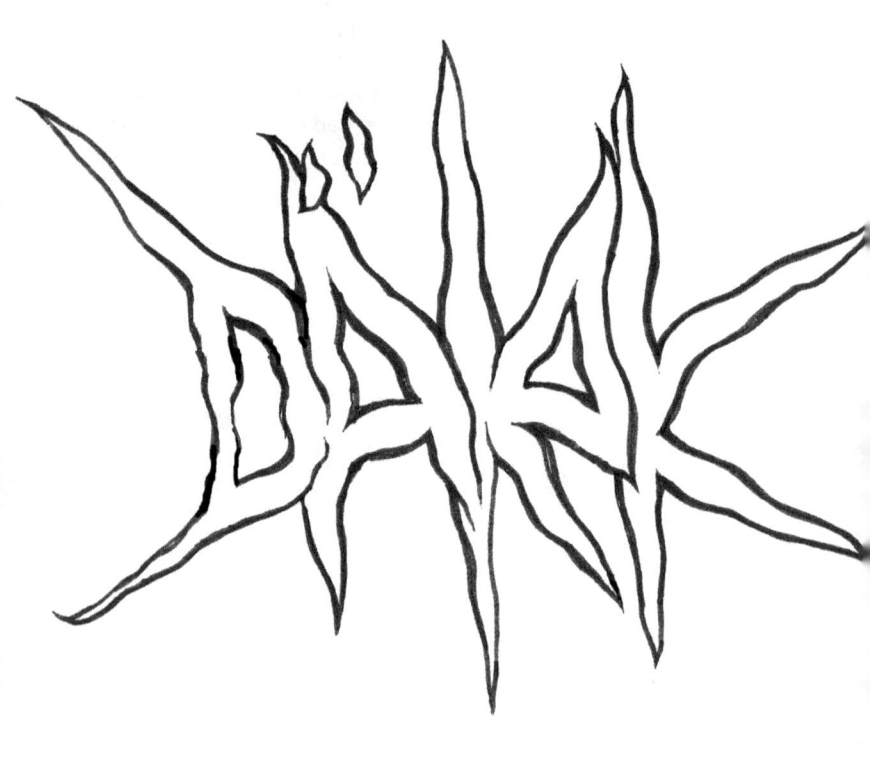

18

dälek
Build and Destroy

Interview and illustration by Roy Christopher
September 30, 2011

"I remember distinctly my first impression of him," Henry Miller once described his first meeting beat writer and poet Kenneth Patchen, "it was that of a powerful, sensitive being who moved on velvet pads." My first meeting Will Brooks of dälek gave me a similar impression. Miller continues,

> I feel that it would give him supreme joy to destroy with his own hands all the tyrants and sadists of this earth together with the art, institutions, and all the machinery of everyday life which sustain and glorify them. He is a fizzing human bomb ever threatening to explode in our midst. … There is almost an insanity to his fury and rebellion.

Brooks embodies these two extremes of Patchen: sensitive to a fault, deeply feeling the pain of his people, but ready to deliver retribution with no quarter and no question. Their poetry comes from the same place, a place of pure protest, pure passion.

For the past decade and a half, Brooks has been the center of one of my favorite bands, the noisy, hip-hop crew dälek. He and Brother Oktopus have roamed the globe, destroying expectations and eardrums. Their blend of drones, feedback, and banging beats often buried the vocals in the mix. Theirs was a united front, as much wall-of-sound as it was words-of-wisdom.

This year Brooks emerged with a solo project. Under the name iconAclass, he's been making noise in his own right but this time around the focus is on the lyrics. The beats are still banging, and the grooves are still deep, but the vocals are given center stage.

Henry Miller called Kenneth Patchen, "a sort of sincere assassin," and I would say the same of Brooks. Allow him to reintroduce himself.

ROY CHRISTOPHER: *Tell me about iconAclass. How does this project differ from dälek? What's the goal?*

WILL BROOKS: Basically, iconAclass is my solo project. Written, produced, and mixed by my own hand. Shit, I even directed, filmed, and edited the videos! The only thing I didn't do were the cuts. Those duties fell to longtime collaborator DJ Motiv. This project is something I wanted to do for a while now. I wanted to do a very stripped-down, Hip-hop project where the lyrics were front and center. I also wanted the challenge of doing a project completely on my own. It was a lot of work, but I am very proud of the final result. The goal, as always, was to make the best possible songs I can make. This is a project that is representative of where my head is at, at this moment. It's that plate of rice and beans, you know? It was that nourishment, that truth that I needed.

RC: *Lyrically, you're still keeping things rough and rugged, exploring similar themes to previous projects. Is this just more of a straight-up hip-hop vibe?*

WB: Yeah, definitely more "traditional," I guess, but of course the lyrics got to be truth. I really don't know any other way to approach music. Again, I definitely wanted to make the lyrics a focal point, whereas in the group dälek, the lyrics were more of an instrument and under-layers of sonics. In today's musical climate, I wanted to remind heads what hip-hop is all about. I feel that production is very innovative in today's music, but there isn't a premium placed on lyricism. Don't get me wrong, there are heads that are still killing it on the mic — Random Axe, Slaughterhouse, Joell Ortiz on his own, Immortal technique, Pete Rock with Smiff n Wesson, Shabazz Palaces, Doh Boi, LONESTARR, John Morrison, just to name a few. I'm just proud to be a part of that hip-hop underground that still has love for the culture and the craft.

RC: *So, I have to ask: What's the status of dälek the group?*

WB: We are currently on hiatus. After fourteen years of doing it, I think both Okotpus and myself needed a break. We are still working on film scores together, we just finished one for a flick called *Lilith,* and running the recording studio together but will be focusing on our respective projects — iconAclass and MRC Riddims — for the time being.

RC: *I'm stoked on the book. What made you finally put your lyrics to paper for mass consumption?*

WB: Back in 2002, William Hooker first suggested I put my lyrics in book form. I guess that planted the seed. While working on this project, graphic artist and longtime friend, Thomas Reitmayer, who worked on the iconAclass album art, approached me with the idea of doing a book of my lyrics with some of his work. I thought it would be a cool thing to press up and have for the first iconAclass tour. It kind of built from there. Adam Jones from Tool was gracious enough to write the foreword, and we got some heads like Prince Paul and Joachim Irmler from Faust to contribute quotes. I was really humbled to have those guys be involved. I'm really proud of the final product. I just wish there were still bookstores these days! [Laughs.]

RC: *Will you be blessing the States with a tour?*

WB: We are hoping to at least set up east and west coast runs in the US in 2012. Would also love to play SXSW next year and Chicago. The logistics of a full US tour are very daunting, but we will make something happen for sure.

RC: *What else is coming up?*

WB: Been running the deadverse recordings record label with my label manager JR Fritsch. We released the deadverse massive *TakeOver* album. We got an iconAclass enhanced EP coming out in November, along with new releases by Oddateee, Dev-One, MRC Riddims, and EPs from Gym Brown, D.L.E.MM.A, and Skalla slated for 2012 and 2013. We are also planning on re-releasing *Negro, Necro, Nekros* (1998) in time for its fifteen-year anniversary. I have also been DJing on *deadverseTV* as well as *Mixcloud*. I've been running a monthly deadverse night at a spot in Brooklyn called Don Pedros. It's been a lot of fun. Basically just the crew and affiliates DJing and performing everything from hip-hop to House and Electro beats. Okto and I got a couple more film scores in the works to look out for. I'm definitely hitting the road heavy in support of iconAclass. And in the midst of all that, I did a couple of remixes for Black Heart Procession and Zombi, as well as some guest appearances and collaborations. Some of the collabs that are in the works are a project with Interpol drummer Sam Fogarino, a possible project with myself, Oktopus, Adam Jones from Tool, and Heitham Al-Sayed, and I also might work on something with Joachim Irmler from Faust and Alec Empire. So, I've been a little busy...

19

MATTHEW SHIPP
Heavy Meta

Interview by Roy Christopher
Illustration by Eleanor Purcell
September 22, 2011

In the 1980s, professional skateboarder Mark Gonzales used to disappear from media coverage for months at a time and every time he would return, he'd introduce the next, new trick. Once it was the kickflip, once the stalefish, but he always set off a new trend. Antipop Consortium have cut a similar path. Their records are few and far between, but they always bump the bar a bit higher than it was before. Their 2002 record *Arrhythmia* (Warp) set the tone for twenty-first century metaphysical hip-hop, and after a seven-year hiatus, *Fluorescent Black* (Big Dada, 2009) re-established what had been lost on heads in the meantime. Oddly abrasive to your expectations and undeniably smart in their creation are the way they work. Intelligent, innovative, and insightful are the watchwords.

The same can be said for Matthew Shipp, William Parker, and Thirsty Ear Recordings. The latter's Blue Series, which includes collaborations with the former, as well as El-P, DJ Spooky, Dave Lombardo, Guillermo E. Brown, Vijay Iyer, and Mike Ladd, among many others, has consistently pushed the boundaries of jazz, hip-hop, and the expectations of all those involved. In

2003, it was as a part of this series that Matthew Shipp, William Parker, and Antipop Consortium previously met. Their aptly titled *Antipop Consortium vs Matthew Shipp* record sounds more like tension than balance, and it is on this tension that the grooves on their self-titled second outing, a collaboration with William Parker, as well as Beans and High Priest from Antipop Consortium, *Knives From Heaven,* rely. Sometimes it sounds like the jostling of traffic swirling around you. Sometimes it sounds like dishes tumbling down stairs. Sometimes it sounds like the incessant churn of machinery. Sometimes it sounds like planets locked in wobbly orbit. No matter: it always sounds just like the future.

I first heard Shipp on the David S. Ware Quartet's *Dao* (Homestead, 1995). I'd gotten review copies of that, William Parker's *Compassion Seizes Bed-Stuy* (1996), and William Hooker's *Armageddon* (1995), which I was planning to review together for *Pandemonium! Magazine* of which I was then editor. Though I submerged myself in these three records and several similar releases, *The Rocket*'s Steve Duda beat me to the review, and I never wrote mine. My taste for the fringes of progressive jazz had been expanded though, and I've checked in with these folks on a regular basis since.

Matthew Shipp not only plays, composes, and collaborates on jazz's edges, but he also thinks deeply about all of the above. When I heard *Knives From Heaven,* I knew it was time to get the man on the line.

ROY CHRISTOPHER: *This isn't the first time you've been in the studio with these guys. How'd you end up working with Antipop Consortium in the first place?*

MATTHEW SHIPP: Beans used to work at a record store here in New York City, and I used to talk to him. He approached me before I had ever heard them. Of course when I heard them, I was blown away by their forward-looking aesthetic.

RC: *What is it about their work that attracts you to collaborate?*

MS: There is nothing cliché about how they go about it, and it has the feel of the same modern, New York zeitgeist that informs my own work.

RC: *Are there any other hip-hop acts you'd like to work with?*

MS: Not really. I used to want to do something with Madlib, and I used to want to work with Kool Keith/Dr. Octagon, but I am completely involved in my own jazz universe now.

RC: *Hip-hop has flirted with jazz regularly over the past twenty years, but the opposite hasn't been the case.* Knives From Heaven *(again) illustrates the untapped potential of their mating. How do you see elements from the two genres working together?*

MS: Well, first I am not sure if *Knives From Heaven* is hip-hop flirting with jazz or jazz flirting with hip-hop —

RC: *I'd say it's both.*

MS: Well, first, music is music, and if you melt down the particulars there is room for dialogue between the various so-called genres. I think the so-called freedom of jazz can be a point of inspiration for certain hip-hop artists of a certain mental bent, and both musics have their own particular swing: The pulse of Free Jazz is a vortex of information, and all electronic musics thrive off of information. Therefore it is up to the imagination and talent of the producer to cook a good meal. The palettes of both musics are different in some respects and similar in some ways so a good cook will figure out a blend that makes sense.

RC: *Your work blends the architecture of composition with the spontaneity of improvisation. How does your process manifest songs? How do you decide where to start versus where to stop?*

MS: I am always working or thinking about my musical language, so how do you start a sentence when you talk? Well, you know the language so well that you just start with the faith that words will come to you that match some internal imagery and the words will match whatever vague emotions and feelings you want to get across to the person you are talking to. It is very similar in this. Also, the deeper you get into your language the deeper the merger between form and content is which means if you have a deep organic concept. The architecture of composition and the spontaneity of improvisation will merge because they come from the same matrix, and form and content are one actuality, so there is some impetus that grows the structure of the piece or improvisation together with the content. And as far as stopping, that is instinct: if you know your language and your phrasing and your flow, you know when the ideas have played themselves out, therefore you know when to shut the fuck up.

RC: *You bend time by mixing tradition with futurism. Do you see music in terms of eras?*

MS: Yes and no. I see music as vibration that emits pulse and coheres in different ways. I see eras as each time period has its own constructs and organizational worldview. I don't really believe in linear time, so eras are an illusion to me, but a very real illusion: every so-called time period has its own questions it asks of vibrations. But I do melt down all so-called time periods in jazz to find some language that I can proceed to move into timeless period in.

RC: *You've been making music long enough to have seen the changes in the technologies of recording and releasing, as well as listening and consuming. Are things getting better or are they getting worse?*

MS: Worse. The world is too complex for its own good. There are too many possibilities and with the proliferation of all the technology and possibilities that we have, with all that, people are no smarter. In fact, you could argue that they are dumber and operate with less focus and concentration about what is really real.

20

TYLER, THE CREATOR
The Odd Future Is Now

Interview by Timothy Baker
Illustration by Roy Christopher
August 17, 2010

A few weeks back I was introduced to a new collective out of Los Angeles called Odd Future Wolf Gang Kill Them All (OFW-GKTA). After a few minutes of watching their videos, I had to pick my jaw up off the ground and hunt down whatever music of theirs I could. Listening to them, it felt like a changing of the guard. It was the same feeling I had when I first heard Suicidal Tendencies self-titled album all those years ago. After listening to *BASTARD* by VMA Best New Artist, Tyler, The Creator, and *EARL* by Earl Sweatshirt, I knew I needed to track these guys down and find out more. Everywhere I went they seemed to be a bit of an enigma. Everyone loved their music, but nobody knew anything about them other than that they were excessively skilled at their craft, offered an excitingly fresh perspective to the stale-as-a-zombie-fart hip-hop scene, and they were young.

TIMOTHY BAKER: *Introduce yourself to the readers, tell them a bit about your history, how you came up, etc.*

TYLER, THE CREATOR: I'm Tyler, I sell weed to minors, and I make music in my spare time. I came up in a very big family: mother was a teacher, father was a firefighter, little sister, and my dog Steve. I took piano lessons at the young age of 7 and started writing poems at 10.

I'm lying. I have no father. My mother was single parent till I was 15. When she bounced up north without me, I taught myself piano at 14 and started rapping at 7 because I fucking sucked at sports.

TB: *OFWGKTA is the collective. Give us a brief introduction to each of the members of the group.*

TTC: Tyler, The Creator's The Head Drug Dealer. Wolf Haley is the evil voice in his head. Hodgy Beats is his right-hand man, along with his brother Left Brain. Earl Sweatshirt is Tyler's young brother, dealing drugs to the younger crowd. Domo Genesis handles the money. And Mike G is the look out.

TB: *How did you guys come together?*

TTC: Most of us met in school and just skating around, selling drugs, and doing real bad hoodrat shit

TB: *Since we all are creations of our influences, how would you describe your sound and how do you feel they come across in the music you create?*

TTC: My sound is like a mosh pit at a jazz concert. Or like Hitler fucking Dr. Suess.

TB: *I saw you listed Ariel Pink's* Haunted Graffiti *as one of your favorite groups, which is also one of my favorite albums this year. What other new artists are you checking for?*

TTC: Ariel's pretty old, but overall I'm fucking with Toro y Moi, the new Nite Jewel EP Is swagged-out, and those Odd Future guys are fucking legit. And I love Justin Bieber.

TB: *As a larger group I'm sure the creative process is a bit rougher than a solo artist or a duo. How does it work for you guys?*

TTC: Well for one, we're all solo artists. We just run together, and we just let shit flow. The first thing that comes to our heads goes down on paper or on a keyboard. We're lucky that people like the shit.

TB: *You mention a few times on* BASTARD *that you don't get fucked up. Is there any reason behind that? Have you gone straight edge like Ian MacKaye?*

TTC: I don't need drugs — except for Albuterol, Prednisone, and Ritalin.

TB: *One of the things I found most refreshing about you guys is that you tend to thumb your nose at the establishment, the forty-year-old rappers talking about how much money they have, etc. How have you found the response to be from established artists?*

TTC: I don't know… Probably when I make a lot of fucking money, I'll buy rims and chains and all that dumb shit, so, if you look at it, I'm a hypocrite-in-progress.

TB: *Most of the people I talk hip-hop with are old fucks like myself who got really into the music during the late 1980s and early '90s. They all seem to share the opinion that hip-hop has gotten boring as shit. There are no real risk takers. Everyone falls into one of like five sounds. It's not even that dudes are technically bad, they are just boring. It would be interesting to get the opinion of a younger artist, especially one who is making the type of music we have all been craving — those same old fucks that bitch non-stop are geeked on you guys and the energy and vibe you bring.*

TTC: Music sucks now. The only rap shit out now that's fucking swag is Waka Flocka, Lil B, and OFWGKTA. Seriously.

TB: *Where do you see it all going? You guys are obviously a self-contained unit with tons of talent. The videos are fresh, the music is great, there is a lot of talk in the music and the videos of skating, even sponsorships. What does the future hold for Odd Future?*

TTC: Who the fuck knows… I want a Grammy, a nice house, trampoline, mini ramp, a cat named Wolf, a lifetime supply of bacon and Cinnamon Toast Crunch — and motor scooters for all my friends. In order to do that I have to work hard and stop jacking off and yelling at people I don't know… and work hard…er.

21

TRICIA ROSE
Hip-Hop Warrior

Interview by Roy Christopher
Illustration by Eleanor Purcell
May 16, 2009

Tricia Rose is the O.G. Hip-Hop Scholar. Her book *Black Noise* (Wesleyan, 1994) is one of the germinal texts for serious hip-hop studies. Anyone who approaches the culture of hip-hop from a serious stance must contend with Rose's work. Her latest book, *The Hip-Hop Wars* (Basic Civitas, 2008), is a critical look at the debates surrounding hip-hop, debates that have largely sprung up in the fifteen years since Black Noise was published. Hip-hop music and culture deserves to be taken seriously and looked at critically, and Tricia Rose is down to give it its due.

ROY CHRISTOPHER: *Tell us a bit about your new book* The Hip-Hop Wars *and how it differs from* Black Noise.

TRICIA ROSE: *Black Noise* was a very academic treatment of the emergence of hip-hop and its political and aesthetic and social element and impact on black culture and US society. It was about the music and lyrics and the social context. Although it addressed the debates about hip-hop in the public sphere it was interested in figuring out hip-hop "on its own terms" and setting an intellectual agenda for understanding what was then an emergent art form.

The Hip-Hop Wars is about the public conversation on hip-hop and how that conversation along with the spiraling downward content of commercial hip-hop is working together to restore racial stereotype — and, therefore undermine real cross-racial unity and equality — dumb down hip-hop fans, and continue the justification of unjust social policies that most negatively impact poor Black youth. It is highly accessible, created with bite size chapters and is intended to spark youth engagement with social justice issues through hip-hop (e.g., gender, race, and class) and to challenge all the stupid arguments leveled for and against hip-hop in mainstream and hip-hop media.

RC: *Can you briefly explain the "gangsta-pimp-ho trinity" and how you think it came about?*

TR: This is a term I came up with to describe the intensely defended most powerful hip-hop triangle of financially profitable but socially destructive images that have dominated commercial mainstream hip-hop for over a decade now. I wanted to convey their mutual relationships, and I wanted to imply that together they make up the "god" of hip-hop that is worshipped by record company executives, rappers (present and aspiring), and fans. I also wanted to challenge readers into thinking about how too many of us invest in these images as if they are the truth, and that anyone who challenges this is considered outside of the culture and therefore unworthy of serious consideration. As for how it came about, well, that's an answer far too long for this space but in *Hip-Hop Wars*! But the very, very short answer would be the a) long and powerful history of racial stereotypes that perceive Blacks as violent, criminal, and hyper sexual but are now refashioned for the urban present; b) expansion of street economies in poor communities due to chronic and very high levels of joblessness that elevates these icons in real life; 3) economic value of these images of Black people.

RC: *I agree with you that the Hip-hop Generation needs "the sharpest critical tools to survive and thrive," but, as Jay-Z says, they just wanna hear their boy talk fly. How are we to engage hip-hop heads with the necessary critique of this dear culture?*

TR: Black youth have always wanted to hear fly artists talk, style, and boast. The issue is not about the style of hip-hop but its content. Black artists have been incredibly creative without elevating the worst of ourselves, without constant justification of self and community destructive attitudes and behaviors. The whole history of jazz is about fly artists talking — think of the powerful style and linguistic and musical creativity associated with BeBop. And politics has always been conveyed through fly talk. What has happened is that now, this style, this powerful way of making creative pleasure is serving a death imperative. It is what I call "the manipulation of the funk," funk serving here as a parallel to the idea of fly boy talk; the role of stylistic pleasure in making content pleasurable.

So, the question isn't why aren't mainstream rappers political (they are — it is a politics of renegade, community destruction) or how do we get them to be critical (they are critical of all kinds of things, but too often it's the wrong things!) it is what kind of politics are some rappers pushing when their "fly boys talk." What kind of critical So the opposite of "bitches ain't nothing but hos and tricks" or "99 Problems" isn't necessarily Public Enemy's "Fight the Power" or Immortal Technique's "The Cause of Death," it is something like Lupe Fiasco's "Kick, Push" or "The Cool" or Common's "The Corner."

RC: *I've asked a few emcees why when one performs angry black music that the audience is mostly white. The answer I get is that it's a class issue not a race issue. That is, middle- and upper-class folks are the ones with the leisure time to contemplate such issues. Other factors notwithstanding do you think this is an accurate assessment of the situation?*

TR: When I watched 50 Cent's DVD concert in the Detroit area,

I was stunned to see the mostly white audience when the rear stage cameras were in action. Yes, middle class youth have both the comfort and the educational resources to attend to these issues in a conceptual way and their consumption of radical ideas is given more room and safety. Black rappers with "angry" political content rapping to an all-black crowd tends to bring out the police and the FBI; there is a long history of that in hip-hop alone, not to mention R&B and Soul music in the late 1960s. And, Black fans use "local" black radio as a key means for guiding consumption. Black radio, which isn't local or black-owned too much anymore, rarely plays radical political content, which would make it seem organic to black communities, which it is, and give it currency among black youth.

RC: *Is there anything else I didn't bring up or that you're working on that you'd like to mention?*

TR: Thanks for asking this. I want to mention the end of the book where I offer six guiding principles for progressive consumption generally and specifically for hip-hop. I think it is so important to remind ourselves of how powerful, energizing, and beautiful creative expression can be. And, to not be manipulated into thinking that the content need not be rough to be valuable (often a culturally conservative position) or that it is "keepin' it real" when it panders to subcultures of self-destruction and violence (the hyper-pro-hip-hop defenders). Most of us need a more balanced and forward looking, progressive way out of this. My six principles outline a larger way to think about culture, our past, our communities and our politics in ways that honors the complexity of creativity but refuses to give a free pass to those who let the market rule. So, I'll close on one of these principles: we live in a market economy, don't let the market economy live in us."

22

SEAN PRICE
Bless the M.I.C.

Interview and illustration by Roy Christopher
May 12, 2009

Sean Price is that dude. He is one-half of "Da Incredible Rap Team" Heltah Skeltah, where he is known as Ruck, one-fifth of the Fab Five, and has been in the Boot Camp Clik since day square. All of that notwithstanding, his solo work is where he truly shines. On *Monkey Barz* (Duck Down, 2005), he proved he could go for solo and drop ill bars with no backup. On *Jesus Price Superstar* (Duck Down, 2007), he proved he was one of the best doing it. He is an emcee who realizes the power of writing, but who doesn't take himself too seriously.

He has several new projects in the works, not the least of which are a record with Guilty Simpson and Black Milk, called Random Axe, and a new solo joint called Mic Tyson.

Admittedly, Sean Price is also my favorite emcee, so it was an extreme honor to catch up with him and ask him a few questions.

ROY CHRISTOPHER: *Emcees are constantly coming cookie-cutter or trying to be so different that they come off corny. You always come different, but you stay in the frame. What keeps you grounded?*

SEAN PRICE: I don't know, and I think not knowing is the key for me.

RC: *Do you have any set goals with your music? If so, what are they?*

SP: Just to put it out and work it really. I don't give a fuck about the best-rapper shit even though I'm pretty good.

RC: *You've been busy, Sean. Tell me about the new joints you have coming up.*

SP: Yeah, I just completed my mixtape entitled *Kimbo Price*. It's just me rhyming on some instrumentals. It's a warm-up to *Mic Tyson*.

Random Axe is me, Guilty Simpson and my G, Black Milk. That's gonna be an incredible album. Black Milk is one of the best producers/emcees in the game. Fire!

RC: *No question… You've been very supportive of hip-hop legends that don't always get support these days (e.g., Das-EFX, Sadat X, and others). How can we get the younger heads to pay homage?*

SP: I don't know, but these younger motherfuckers better respect they elders!

I'm a fan of hip-hop, first of all. I was one of those kids who taped Red Alert and Mr. Magic and Marley Marl. I copped LPs and read the credits so when I got a deal later, it was an honor for me to be surrounded by motherfuckers I grew up listening to, and I stay humble. I remember smoking a blunt with Primo watching him work on "Unbelievable" for Biggie. Ah, good times.

RC: *What else are you working on?*

SP: A lot of shit like the Ill Bill/Sean P. LP called *The Pill*, and a surprise LP with — Stay tuned!

Oh, I was kicked out the group La Coka Nostra; they ain't wanna deal with my kind. I said, "what kind do you mean?" And Lefty round-house kicked me in the stomach, and Ill Bill did his best King Kong Bundy impersonation. Lawsuits pending. Letahl didn't want me in the group because he signed Rock and didn't wanna deal with me. Lawsuits pending.

RC: *Is there anything else you'd like to bring up here?*

SP: Nah. Just keep God in ya life, and you be ah'ight.

23

RAMMELLZEE
The Wrath of the Math

Interview by Chuck Galli
Illustration by Roy Christopher

The following correspondences were collected as part of a senior honors, BA thesis in African and African-American studies titled *Hip-Hop Futurism: Remixing Afrofuturism and the Hermeneutics of Identity* that I wrote in 2008 and 2009 at Rhode Island College in Providence, Rhode Island. In the course of my research I came upon RAMMELLZEE and his impressive body of art, writing, and interviews concerning the future. I contacted him through his website and asked if he would be willing to answer a few prepared questions through email that I had for him. He agreed and even responded to some follow-up questions.

Part I: October 12, 2008

CHUCK GALLI: *Alondra Nelson writes that "Afro Futurism arises out of an engagement of dispersed people with technology," and Patrick Neate notes that hip-hop is unique in its exclusive reliance on technology for production. How has technology informed Gothic Futurism and/or Ikonoklast Panzerism?*

RAMMELLZEE: There is no such thing as Afro Futurism. Because of Sun Ra, George Clinton, Bootsy Collins, and the 5% Nation are our view on thoughts of Futurism. A time table has become Mapamatical. Weapons technology and the Alpha Bet system, the A was dropped from Beta, concludes the Barbarian that I am. These secrets are of "the Hidden." Black as a culture has nothing to do with it. The Romans stole it from the Greeks. And we still instill it. Language dies. The Hueman species also does. You will run out of genes shortly… I suggest space travel for you. Then you may extend your life expectancy… or you will all die from cancer from inter-breeding.

CG: *Would your ideas on Gothic Futurism and Ikonoklast Panzerism have come about had the hip-hop culture/phenomenon never happened?*

R: [Laughs.] The Gothics and Futurism are two different subjects. It takes one of fourteen, maybe fifteen people that I know of in my life span that dare think and tear apart them both. Those who refuse this thought of thinking… may not like what they find. For us, the idea is to get you and your readers to cellulize… what is the most fundamental. I can be wrong… but that's all right… I have not graduated from school. I am a school. I was never taught, but it seems you have to be. All the better, I was never trained for schooling. But you will be… good and bad for you!

CG: *Author Paul Gilroy writes that a major difference between the future-oriented writings of prominent Black authors and white authors is the importance that Black authors give to "the jubilee" over "the utopia." In other words, African-American writings are more often concerned with a life/the world/the universe culminating in a flare of just-ness and righteousness, regardless of the material destruction, than humankind achieving a utopia in the modernist, materialist, rationalist sense. Do you think humanity will or can reach a material utopia? What does a jubilee look like to you?*

R: There's no difference between a white and a Black author. Astonishment... called "universe" cancels itself out to the conclusion known as "Transversus." As a quantum physicist, time has no meaning. Dimension is of a sum known as the equation 1 over n, n over 1.

CG: *At the risk of coming off as an essentialist, I'm curious: do you believe there is anything about "the Black experience" that gives Blacks certain special tools in futuristic thinking and construction?*

R: No. Where do us as a people get off thinking that we, because we are the oldest of people, have dominated anyone's belief that we are the dominants or dominators of the Hueman species? And why do you care?

CG: *You mention popes, Roman law, and Gothic script, which are mostly products of European civilization, in your treatise and other writings quite frequently. To what extent, if any, do non-European histories, especially African, inform your thinking?*

R: The formula for any language, slanguage, and dialect is for war to conquer, enslave, and control... and most importantly... to police. And last, but not sure, to seize.

CG: *You deal primarily with the Roman alphabet in your writings on Ikonoklast Panzerism, though you also mention the importance of Arabic, Hebrew, Chinese, Mayan, and other valid languages. To your knowledge is there anyone arming these other alphabets? If so, will there be inter-alphabetic confrontations in the future? If there is no one arming these, will Roman eclipse other alphabets?*

R: Only if I start it. And that day may come. But it will be in the middle of the night... and boy... you better be awake.

CG: *You mentio ned in your "Yearly Conclusional" posted on your website that you were once down with the Five-Percenters but left them in 1979. What caused you to break with them?*

R: This answer is of "the Hidden."

CG: *How does your music act as a vehicle for, or contribute to, your futuristic thinking?*

R: I'm a method actor.

CG: *Why should humans bother thinking about the future beyond their lifetimes if they will not live to see it?*

R: The genetic code of the species does not dictate past tense. It allows us to dream. Futures think for us. In time, some of us, stay awake longer than most... and that is "ism." We do not dream. We do not nightmare. We simply view. As a musician, it is hard to think for myself. I can make policy... but then, I have a wife. I have to be tolerated. Then with course, if paid enough, I'll do what I want.

CG: *Do you believe there is an absolute truth (God/s, universal law, unchanging physics, absolute morality, etc.)?*

R: No! There is Alpha Positive and Lord's Minus. They're the implosion/explosion of Mapamatics. The design of the Transversus and time has no tables... it is like a glass that doesn't leak water... but still sticks to the tray.

Part II: October 27, 2008

CG: *You wrote to me that "the genetic code of the species [Hueman] does not dictate past tense. It allows us to dream." What, if any, relevancy does history hold for humans? Is history a crucial part of our lives or an idle obsession?*

R: As forth, with the policing of the Hueman species, deliberates essential politics for the digestion of the common man or wombed-man. Genetic code is your Reaper Grimm.

CG: *You gave an emphatic "no!" to the question as to whether or not a universal truth exists and referred to the "Transversus." Can you elaborate on this theory and give an example of what is possible in the Transversus that is not possible in the "universe"?*

R: First of all, uni cannot verse itself, in the equation as its own usage in quantum physics "string" theory applies in vibration as re-verberation. Transversus does not vibrate… it is a membrane of the womb. It expands and contracts… as your "so called" universe does.

CG: *After the Roman letters are armed and begin fighting, do you think any of them will be destroyed?*

R: All of them! Language, slanguage, dialects of all Earth's icons. But there is one more possibility… in less than 200 years… 4 more letters will be added to the Alpha Bet — a call! End of period! It will be no longer… AD… it will be AE meaning After Extinction of the planet Earth.

CG: *What are your thoughts on human war? How do you see human war (bad, good, inevitable, pointless, etc.)?*

R: The good and the bad… share each other. You call me an Afro Futurist… I am of the Gothics.

24

CADENCE WEAPON
Check the Technique

Interview by Roy Christopher
Illustration by Laura Persat
June 7, 2008

I am hereby requesting a bandwagon late-pass. Out of nowhere a few months ago, someone sent me the video for "Sharks" by Cadence Weapon. Like many who've heard the track, I was instantly hooked and started looking for more. Well, lucky me, Cadence Weapon had just put out a new disc of his glitchy hip-hop called *Afterparty Babies* (Anti-, 2008). It's been in or near the top of the playlist ever since.

Before dropping the bubbly beats and fresh rhymes, Cadence Weapon, a.k.a. Rollie Pemberton, used to write reviews for a major music website, but, way before that, his dad was Edmonton, Alberta's premiere source for hip-hop. At age thirteen, Rollie knew he wanted to rap, and his starting young is evident in the work: his records — though he's only been making them for a few years — are those of a veteran. He's grown up with this ish. It's in his bloodstream.

Clever and catchy hip-hop that doesn't outsmart itself might be more prevalent now than ever, but it still isn't lurking on every airwave. I'm glad to pass the name Cadence Weapon on to you. He gets respect for the rep when he speaks. Check the technique, and see if you can follow it.

ROY CHRISTOPHER: *Tell me about the new record. What's different this time around?*

CADENCE WEAPON: This record is faster paced, more cohesive, and tied to a connecting concept. It's more personal and drawing from more dancefloor influences than IDM or grime.

RC: *Your dad was a hip-hop pioneer up there in Edmonton. What are your earliest impressions of hip-hop and music?*

CW: I grew up on rap music and culture, so I just saw it as normal. Predictably, I was isolated not knowing many other people who were into rap music, so it was just something I liked myself. I saw it as an extension of poetry or any other artistic expression, and I still do.

RC: *Though hip-hop as a genre is often innovative and rebellious, it's also steeped in strict traditions and rules. What's your take on this contradiction — and negotiating it as an artist?*

CW: It's one of the strangest things about the music. It's the most open-ended genre in terms of possibilities. You can sample someone walking down the street and rap about your mom's hat if you wanted to because there are no constraints in rap, just the ones built by the individual. The regimented nature of rap is a response to its corporate status: people thinking you have to maintain the status quo to retain sales. It's shitty.

RC: *Comedian David Spade once said that acts spend the first part of their career looking for a hook and the rest of it trying to bury that hook. To me, this is analogous to one having a "hit" (e.g., De La Soul's "Me, Myself, and I" or, more recently, Aesop Rock's "No Regrets"). Do you ever resent the attention you got from "Sharks"?*

CW: The success of "Sharks" doesn't bother me. As with any single, it's seen as representative of who I was at the time of its release. It's a catchy song, it's youthful and aggressive and not necessarily who I am right now, but I accept it as a period in my life. I am not trying to get rid of the memory of that song, I feel like there are still layers to it that people haven't necessarily uncovered.

RC: *What's next for Rollie Pemberton? And for Cadence Weapon?*

CW: Next for Rollie Pemberton: making the most of my free time, playing basketball, getting back into party mode, bettering myself.

Next for Cadence Weapon: actually collaborating with people on my next album, writing about death and body image and the other side of the world, starting a band, rapping harder.

25

EL-P
Wake Up. Time to Die.

Interview by Roy Christopher
Illustration by Laura Persat
March 15, 2007

I'm a child of the '80s when, as emcee/producer/label-owner El-Producto puts it, every hip-hop record that came out was that new sound, that next shit. As you all know, I'm still a huge hip-hop fan, but those new styles just don't drop that often, much less with every new release. Now typically someone hits it big with a style and others scramble to sound the same. Not so with El-P. His musical M.O. is from that previous era where you had to innovate or you fell off, and biting was not allowed or tolerated under any circumstances.

Also reared on '80s music and culture, El's apocalyptic boom-bap bounces between the frenetic cut-and-paste of the early Bomb Squad and the off-world synths and sounds of The Art of Noise — perhaps taking its initial cues from a collision of *It Takes a Nation of Millions* and *In Visible Silence*. From there, only one thing is guaranteed: the drums will be bangin'. All other bets are hedged.

Therefore, it's no surprise that the drums on his new record, *I'll Sleep When You're Dead* (Def Jux, 2007) are bangin', but the guests along for the ride might surprise some people. In the mix are friends and fellow travelers Trent Reznor, Chan Marshall, members of TV on the Radio, The Mars Volta, and Yo La Tengo, as well as Def Jux fam Aesop Rock and Cage with cuts by the mighty Mr. Dibbs and DJ Big Wiz. Don't let the names overwhelm you though. This is El's record from jump to stop.

It's been four years since we've gotten an El-P LP proper, but, to be fair, El has been busy behind the boards producing and remixing for the likes of Del the Funky Homosapien, Prefuse73, TV on the Radio, Nine Inch Nails, Slow Suicide Stimulus, and fellow Def Jukies Cage Kennylz, Mr. Lif, S.A. Smash, and others. Oh sure, there was his future-jazz Blue Series Continuum record, *High Water* (Thirsty Ear, 2004), which, along with the Blue Series Continuum crew of Matthew Shipp, Guillermo E. Brown, William Parker, Daniel Carter, Steve Swell, and Roy Campbell, featured his dad Harry Keys on one song. Then there was the eclectic, but consistent, compilation *Collecting the Kid* (Def Jux, 2004), which brought together stray pieces from his soundtrack work on the graff flick *Bomb the System* (Palm Pictures, 2002) with unreleased tracks from his group with Camu Tao, Central Services, among other odds and ends. Aside from a few guest appearances — El has shared tracks with fellow wordsmiths Aesop Rock, The Weathermen, Del, Ghostface Killah, C-Rayz Walz, and Cage — El's fingers have been on the knobs, keys, and buttons, as opposed to the mic, since 2002.

Production credits notwithstanding, El-P is a monster of an emcee. His presence, power, and lyrical prowess on the mic are unmatched. Where other lyricists just bring their next release, he brings the State of the Union. He's Rick Deckard to all of the microphone Replicants out looking for life-extension. There's a reason their lifespans are limited, and El-P retires them all.

Admittedly, I'm more of a fan than a critic, and more of a nerd than a thug, but those tensions are evident in El-P as well. He lives and loves hip-hop but will quickly call bullshit on wackness. He's also mad smart and loves science fiction but won't hesitate to bust you in your shit.

From his days in the germinal 1990s hip-hop crew Company Flow to his current assault on the ears of the jaded, El-Producto is always bringing it rough and rugged. The future is now.

ROY CHRISTOPHER: *You're approaching hip-hop from a different angle than anyone else. What's your take on what you're bringing to it that makes that difference?*

EL-PRODUCTO: Originality... Style... I don't delude myself into thinking that this shit sounds like all the other hip-hop out there. Basically, I pride myself on the fact that it doesn't, but it all comes from a Brooklyn kid who grew up on all the classics, and all of those things are just layered in it. Honestly, if I had to think about it, I'd say I'm bringing some decently needed style to the whole picture. I think that's the cornerstone of my whole shit, and that's why I always look at it as raw hip-hop because that to me is the ultimate purpose.

I grew up learning about hip-hop from writers and break dancers and from really being involved in the culture and the whole shit was about style and having your own twist on it. If you come out sounding like what everyone else is sounding like then you're a toy. So, I filled in from a lot of the traditional shit that I grew up on and the era that I came up in, and underneath it all, underneath the trippy sound is my Ced G influence and my Scott La Rock influence and my Bomb Squad influence. When different cats listen to the record, whatever their background is, a lot of them pick out different things from it. People who are familiar with that and grew up listening to the same stuff I did have an easier time hearing that.

RC: *It's like you've said before about that era, whenever a new record came out that was the new sound.*

EP: Yeah, and somewhere along the line people have grown into this malaise that they've applied to themselves philosophically, and I think it's just that they've stopped being moved by music. I think it's an excuse for people to justify the fact that they've stopped craving to be thrilled. I think it's cynical, and I can't be cynical in my approach to music. I have to always be throwing myself down a flight of stairs hoping that at the bottom of the stairs is what I'm looking for. I don't have that thing in me that tells me to preserve myself and to stop going where I feel I want to go and what I want to hear. I don't have that thing in me that tells me that there's a rule to apply to making a great record — apart from a few things: the drums have to bang. That's the number one, and, for what it's worth, I think I've got that part down.

RC: *No doubt. Ryan Kidwell once said that playing it safe is not interesting.*

EP: Yeah, you start to wonder who you're playing it safe for. The same people who would have you play it safe are the same people who don't want to hear it when you do. The audience and the critical community don't enter into my creative process because I feel like I'm a pretty good representation of a music fan. So, I just go where I have to go. The thing about it is that I know who I am. I was born and raised in New York City and grew up on some ill, B-boy shit, and so this is me. Everything that emanates from me is an extension of that, it's built in. I believe in reference, but I don't believe in imitation. I don't hold on to too much nostalgia because I don't have to.

RC: *You have a lot of guests on this record. Where others just pile 'em on to see what names they can get on their record, your guest spots make sense. How much chance was involved in who showed up on the record and how much was fully planned?*

EP: It was a combination of elements. If you write down all of the names who appear even in the most minor way on the record it looks like it could be some crazy collaboration-style record. The reaction I'm getting from people when they listen to it is that they couldn't necessarily tell who was on the record. Most of the time it's me making songs and trying to come up with some idea and at any given time I might feel that someone that I know or that I'm cool with or in contact with or who's in my circle, friends or peers, I hear their voice somewhere and think that they might be able to add to it, and that's usually when I reach out. The idea is there first, the music is there first, and what I'm trying to do is there first. On this record there was nothing that I did that was created specifically for anyone else to come on, except the song with Cage because we sat down and wrote it together, and the song with Aesop, but that's just on some family rap shit. With all the other guys, I had talked to some of them about the idea—to have the Mars Volta guys, Trent, and Cat Power—about the possibility of me including them. Just so that they would be open if I heard it. And it happened that I really did feel that there were moments that would work with them, and I tried to do it tastefully. I tried to make it so it wasn't some heavy-handed, rock-rap-style thing.

RC: *I got the advance and there's no information about who's on what song, and I couldn't tell at first, except for Cage and Aes because I know those guys.*

EP: Well, you can tell that there are certain parts where it's probably not me. [Laughs.]

RC: *Yeah, but the overall experience is that it's your record.*

EP: Well, good 'cause that was important to me. That's what it was about. This has to be my record. There are moments where there are other voices, but it's almost like I'm sampling. I'm sampling from experience and putting it in at the right time. I think one of the mistakes you can make when you have access to work with some of the guys that you admire is the temptation to use them as much as possible, and that just wasn't what is was about for me.

RC: *It was fun to read about your progress while working on the record.* What prompted your doing the blog?

EP: It was kind of a spontaneous thing. I was sitting around and happened to be looking at different sites on the internet and started bouncing around on some of the random blogs. I started to realize that the majority of these things — really all of them, as different as they all seem to be — they're really all critical blogs. You know, a guy who listens to some music, maybe recommends some of it, and maybe hates some of it. Or film or whatever, but all connected to the critical community, and it doesn't seem like it's connected to the creative community yet — at all. Is there another use for this? It's just a medium that you write things on, why is everyone writing the same things?

So, I just signed up to get my own blog. I've seen how much fans enjoy the interaction being let in, to a degree, on MySpace, message boards, things like that where you can communicate to a degree, but even that is kinda cold. When artists attempt to communicate directly with them on message boards it comes off a little wack because you're always floating in like some sort of other entity, saying things, and then running away. I figured fuck it, why not create an artist's view of the artistic process and let it be public. It will let people in a little bit and see how they dig it. Something that was attached to the creative process, as opposed to a critical process or the sum result of gathering up a bunch of people's art and saying something about it. I didn't know how people would respond to it, but the response was crazy. It was overwhelming, and I kinda feel bad that I stopped doing it, but I'm not a blogger. I'm an artist.

Maybe I'll start it up again. It'll stick around. I was really shocked how much people were into it, but it's kinda like if I were to stumble upon one of my favorite artist's collection of notebooks, all their scribblings and little pictures they'd cut out and put in there, all of that great shit that goes on when artists are in that mode. It's always fun to me. It's always ill to see those things, and I'll even flip through my friend's stuff just because it's interesting to me.

That was the only reason. It wasn't any grand plan. It was just kind of an idea. It just seemed like a natural thing. I'm surprised more people haven't done it.

RC: *Me too, and you and Dibbs had a lot of fun with it, and so did all of us who were reading it.*

EP: I think we'll probably start it up again for the tour.

RC: *I'm a big Alexander Calder fan, so ever since seeing the bird in the art on* Fantastic Damage, *I've wanted to hear the Calder story.*

EP: The details are a little hazy, but basically the story goes that my mother in the '70s — late-'70s perhaps, maybe '78 or '79 — worked with him. She was working in advertising back then, and she worked with him on some project. She was a big fan of his, and she asked him to draw something for her baby, and I was maybe one or two, maybe three, I don't know. He drew this bird for me on this toy wooden airplane that she had bought for me. It's just something that's always been around all my life.

My mother and my father back in the day were highly into art. They were kinda scenesters. They hung out with Robert Crumb. They were into all of that and they were big fans of Calder. So I've had this thing lying around all my life, it's just always been there. It's maybe one thing I still have from my childhood — this drawing on this toy airplane drawn in pencil by this fucking legendary guy. It started to represent me for myself. It's the oldest thing that someone had drawn for me. The more I learned about who he was as I got older, the more interesting it was to me as opposed to being just this thing that I had, but it's old, it's in pencil, it's on wood, and it's fading and eventually it's probably not going to be visible anymore. I figured I'd put it on my body somewhere. I figure if I'm ever super poor I can always lop off my arm, put it in formaldehyde, and auction it off. [Laughs.] So, it's just become a representation of who I am. It's just been there all my life, and it's symbolism that doesn't represent anything else except my life. I like to think of it as some ancient archetypal symbol that represents me.

26

SADAT X
My Protocol Is Know-It-All

Interview by Roy Christopher
Illustration by Josh Row
January 6, 2007

Sadat X is a certified hip-hop legend. The God has been blessing mics since hip-hop's so-called "heyday" with the group Brand Nubian — one of the first groups to bring 5% knowledge to the masses — and he's still doing his thing. His first solo outing, *Wild Cowboys* (Elektra, 1996), proved he could hold his own, *Experience & Education* (Female Fun, 2005) showed he had grown and matured as a man and as an emcee, and his latest, *Black October* (Female Fun/Riverside Drive, 2006), might just be his most consistent, personal, and important record to date. The dense basslines, boom-bappish beats, and of course, Sadat's unmistakable flow all provide a fitting home for his incomparable lyrics. Knowledge and wit come standard, and the day-to-day tales balance fun with the weight of his reality — revealing, without inducing cringes.

I find that I often have to justify my love of hip-hop. Sadat X has been doing hip-hop as long as I've been listening to it. We came up in the same era, but in different environments. We're both old enough to remember when there were no hip-hop records, no hip-hop section in the record store, and certainly no hip-hop groups winning Academy awards.

We touch on all of that and more in the following brief interview, which took place while Sadat was on tour late last year, chilling in a Denver hotel room before a show there. Peace to the God.

ROY CHRISTOPHER: *Where many veterans are chasing that new-school money (having seen the come-ups of Sean Combs, Shawn Carter, Curtis Jackson, et al.), with this record you chose to just do you. What makes that difference?*

SADAT X: First of all, the people around me — my family, my people, my associates — they always had money anyway, before rap, so if I need money, it's there for me. So money was never an issue. I do this here for the love, for the beat, for the drums. I'm just about hip-hop. It was never really a money thing for me.

RC: *I think hip-hop is perfect for the classroom and have tried to incorporate what it has taught me into my teaching as much as possible. Do you see much overlap between your role on the mic and your tasks at the blackboard?*

SX: When I was working in the school system in New Rochelle, I was around a lot of younger kids. So, they didn't know about Brand Nubian, but they would come in saying, "Yo, Mr. Murphy, my father knows you," or "my mother knows you." Music is definitely a big influence on the kids, and I would try to incorporate that into it sometimes.

RC: *You've shown up in some surprising places in recent years, sharing tracks with Hangar 18, Vast Aire, and others. How do you choose whom you work with?*

SX: Different ways. A lot of times, people get in contact with me, or I might contact them, as far as Vast is concerned, I like that cat. He's real unorthodox, plus he's a big dude. He's like a big, cool, teddy bear to me. He's like the coolest, smartest dude that I know, man. I love him to death. I just like his style. And with Hangar 18, we hooked up through a mutual friend.

RC: *Those are my boys. I love those cats.*

SX: Yeah, yeah. They cool, too. I respect that they grind and they struggle, and they reached out to me and wanted me to do something.

RC: *Having been a hip-hop head since day square, you've seen the music go through its every phase firsthand. Does your perspective on the industry make you want to inform the newbies of anything?*

SX: Well, you know, it's the highest-selling form of music out there now, and it is worldwide. I respect these kids that are going out there and getting money off of it, but I don't like kids who aren't being original. When I was coming up, you had rappers like Kool G Rap, Big Daddy Kane, Rakim, De La Soul, and groups like that, and I loved all of them, but I never wanted to emulate them. I always wanted to be my own, have my own voice in this game. Now, a lot of kids are out there makin' money doing the exact same thing that that person is doing.

RC: *And you keep hearing cats wanting to go back to "when hip-hop was great," and I'm like, "what are you listening to? Hip-hop is better now than it's ever been!"*

SX: That's the thing, I knew people who were into hip-hop back then, and now they hate it, and I can't understand it because look at the overall view of hip hop: hip-hop is about forty years old, and we've listening to this music since it started, so now are we supposed to just turn off, just stop listening to it?! That's why I try to make some of my music more mature sometimes — for the older crowd. There's got to be some artists for us too. There's a lot of people over thirty-five that still love hip-hop.

WRITING

27

YTASHA L. WOMACK
Dance to the Future

Interview by Roy Christopher
Illustration by Laura Persat
June 24, 2019

After years of bubbling under the surface of things, Afrofuturism has emerged recently as a cultural force. As with anything that explodes in the mass mind yet has a hidden history, there seems to be some confusion following the movement. Thankfully we have expert guides like Ytasha L. Womack. From her roots as a hip-hop journalist and her deeply researched nonfiction to her dance-therapy practice and her many stellar science fiction stories, Womack is one of the best. I have been fortunate enough to hang out and talk with her on several occasions, and I can say that as bright as her written work shines, she's a straight-up supernova in person.

ROY CHRISTOPHER: *You slide easily among several areas of research and creative practices. For the uninitiated, how would you explain your work?*

YTASHA WOMACK: My work centers around the use of the imagination as a tool of resilience and around the valuing of humanity and community as it relates to culture and identity. If you look at how I talk about Afrofuturism as theory, it centers around the robust nature of imagination in African Diasporic culture. If you look at my fiction and film, you notice themes of identity and community in a very imaginative space. I present dance as a bridge for all these ideas.

I'm a trained dancer and journalist, so much of my work is shaped through that lens. Growing up in dance, I did tap, modern, ballet, African, pom, and hip-hop. As an adult I studied Latin dance including flamenco, samba, and salsa. Through it all I was a house music dancer. As a journalist, I covered mostly business, arts, and entertainment. As a journalist, you look for the untold story, the trend that no one is writing about. And as a person who was well aware of the often-flat coverage of people of the African Diaspora, I was driven to tell these stories and stories of intersectionality with an array of cultures and vantage points. I would note relationships between ideas and then would find myself reading a thousand books to connect the dots… and the fact that I had to read so many different things to get to one point led me to writing books in theory that centralized concepts.

As a journalist, much of my writing was centered around sharing untold stories in the African Diaspora, particularly nuanced stories. The telling of these stories stretched notions of black identity and shifts in identity in general for readers, and this evolved into much of my work centering around Afrofuturism. As a child, I wanted to be an anthropologist or archaeologist, so in many ways I feel like I'm creating artifacts, whether they are news stories or film, for archaeologists of the future to provide some lens into how people now experience their own time. Afrofuturism evolved into a healthy prism for exploring both the past and the future. The discovery of the term helped ground my creative and theory-based work in a way where I could integrate ideas about culture, space, time, and art in ways that better explained myself and also gave a more fluid framework for understanding resilience and fluidity in culture. I grew up in a world where I was very entrenched in Black American culture, urban culture, and multiculturalism. I grew up in metaphysics as a practice.

RC: *You and I have had a similar trajectory from interviews and collections to more theoretical work, but you have also written quite a bit of science fiction. How does writing science fiction inform to your nonfiction writing and vice versa?*

YW: Journalists in many ways are similar to scientists. We're preoccupied with the how and the why and feel charged to get this information out to the world. We're also accustomed to interviewing people and being in the mix of changing spaces. Journalists are also trained to connect with audiences. Much of my theoretical work is influenced by this journalistic temperament. I write from the standpoint of having lived experiences in the communities I'm writing about. I talk to people about their lives. The theories I explore are based more on observation of lived experiences, scores of people working with a set of experiences. I don't write theory from the standpoint of pontificating things I don't see in practice on some level. Nor can I write as if I'm the first person to ever connect a set of dots.

I feel as if people of African descent are not given enough credit for the resilience practices we are already doing or have been doing. People of color and multicultural intersections of society are not always recognized for innovative practices, particularly when they don't fit the dominant narrative. This frustrates me because so many people over time have been innovators and put what they could into practice, and it's downplayed because these actions didn't save the entire world or get heavy coverage in some mainstream publication. Just because it wasn't heavily documented in the mainstream doesn't mean it didn't happen or that it didn't have impact. I tend to write about those things that were innovative, had impact, and laid a groundwork for opportunity today.

I'm very much about application, though I think there's a space for theory for theory's sake. Personally, I feel to write about Afrofuturism as theory you have to have some tangible artistic or scientific practice to inform your insights otherwise the work can only go so far. Afrofuturism bridges the conscious and unconscious mind, and, in my opinion, it's not ideal to rely purely on linear logic to articulate or be informed by it. I began writing science fiction in the midst of writing my *Afrofuturism* book because the experience of exploring the ideas I was writing about demanded that I have a conscious Afrofuturist experience, understanding my personal relationship to it all, in order to finish. That project was the *Rayla 2212* (CreateSpace Publishing, 2014) book, most of which I wrote in the middle of writing *Afrofuturism*. I had other eye-opening experiences with art before, particularly on the dance floor. But writing about the theory created a dynamic where I needed to have a conscious, tangible experience to better inform how I would write the book. I think one of my biggest takeaways from that experience was a very real understanding of the imagination as transformative, the fact that we often have to imagine futures and the past to connect with ourselves.

RC: *Dance is an aspect of hip-hop culture that gets less attention than the other elements, yet it's central to your approach. Can you briefly explain the importance of dance in your work?*

YW: I grew up dancing. Everyone in my family likes dancing. Most of my friends growing up were dancers. I never saw dancing as a big deal. With my family, one of our coming of age moments was learning how to step, a Chicago-based partner dance. You weren't turning 18 without knowing this dance. It was a rite of passage or something. Generally, as kids, we had to show our parents the latest dances, so dance was always a part of the family conversation.

To me, everyone danced or at least they wanted to. As an adult, I had to make very conscious moments to dance, whether that meant taking more classes or going out to dance all the time. Dance was essential. But at some point, I was hanging around friends of mine in metaphysics circles, and when I would talk about dance as, say, a path of enlightenment, they looked at me like I was from *bizarro* world. They literally didn't get it, and I found myself looking for spaces that understood what I was talking about. For them, enlightenment paths were all about stillness and more reading and that just wasn't registering all the time. I was invited to be with a sister circle and the facilitator taught breathing meditations that required movement. This led me to ecstatic dance circles, and I realized there was virtually no difference between ecstatic dance and house music dance except the demographic and often the level of bass and rhythm in the music. I took dance therapy classes. Then I had an opportunity to study dance in Cuba, and the whole idea of specific movements having meaning explained everything my soul was searching for. I gained a really nuanced understanding of why we're all dancing in the first place. So, I started a dance practice for myself one that encouraged freestyle dance. I didn't expect it to go beyond that. I was teaching dance to kids. I created an Afrofuturism Dance Therapy class around the personal practice I created and offered it as a program for adults and teens. I did this because dance is very natural, yet our society has a weird relationship to it.

Increasingly I was in circles where people were freaked out by dance. Black people were freaked out by dance, and it was really absurd to me. Dance is such a central aspect of culture and resilience.

You're at a social event, the lights are down, danceable music is on and nothing about you wants to dance ever? How is that possible? What layered conditioning are you wrapped up in to refuse to move to a beat ever? What's the fear?

Like, you can't just dance to dance. It has to be monetized or for performance. Why can't you just dance because it feels good and you enjoy it? Dance is exoticized and, to some extent, so is the body at large. Significant swaths of society are uncomfortable with core movements from the African Diaspora, as if rotating your hips equates you to being a snake charmer. We're human beings. We're in bodies. But when I work with teens in Afrofuturism Dance Therapy work, they're exposed to a range of dance styles in the African Diaspora, but they also get to do freestyle work. They get a broader understanding of the discipline in dance and the relationships between dance styles, movements, and nature which all help them become more comfortable with their bodies. The point isn't for everyone to be a professional dancer but rather to make dance a part of their life and gain an appreciation for its value to humanity. Ultimately, they see themselves as part of a larger universe and a bridge between times and spaces.

RC: *You seem to use writing residencies to great effect. What do find especially advantageous to these spaces and opportunities?*

YW: I had a residency with Emerson College in Boston. I had an opportunity to teach master's writing classes and to present my work. One of the best things about the residency was listening to students who were really wrestling with ideas in Afrofuturism, culture, or the craft of writing and getting a lens into their perspectives. There were students who felt they were being drawn to write about things, very culturally specific things, and they needed to feel confident that they were on the right path. It was interesting to talk to students who really had a tough time looking US history of the creation of the nations in North and South America as it related to stolen native lands and enslaved African populations square in the face. Or to talk through the resilience/resistance efforts that followed through the Civil Rights Movement to today. You're probably thinking, well what about your writing? As a person who talks about futures, especially in the Afrofuturist context of the future/past/present being one, I have to lay groundwork for the past. Helping people to see themselves as products, not just of their own work or their parents' work, but in part a larger, historical narrative. This grounding creates a shift in paradigm for many hearing it for the first time. They are not alone in the world trying to be this artist; they are part of a story and truth themselves which they need to be cognizant of.

I also had a great residency with Kickstarter. I got really great insights into marketing my project. I also got to bond with other creatives and immerse myself in ontological questions about creativity. I launched the project *A Spaceship in Bronzeville* about Bonnie, a reporter who hangs out with a not-so-secret society of space and paranormal observer geeks in Chicago's Bronzeville in 1951. They're all part of the Great Migration of African Americans who moved North from the South and who are approached by a pansexual pleasure activist from the future who invites them to the future. The project is being published by Mouse Books, which does these phone sized books. The campaign is funded. I wrote the third book during my residency, and I was very conscious of travelling, being in Brooklyn for the residency, and how that was impacting what I wrote. It was probably one of the first times when I was so aware of my real-time life impact on a story. I also had to switch up my writing process because I was travelling a lot. Ultimately, writing residencies force you to be conscious of what you're doing as a writer and why. It compelled me to really be aware of process in a very nuanced way. Writer residencies also make you embrace the fact that you're a writer or creative. If you didn't know before the residency, you certainly know afterwards. At Emerson, when I was advising students on their writing, they could describe moments in their journey, and I knew exactly where they were and how to push past it. Until I had that residency, while I talked a great deal about Afrofuturism, I didn't speak frequently on craft as a writer. The whole experience made me think of myself differently.

Writing residencies made me more conscious of my perspective, what shaped these perspectives, the schools of thought and historical narratives that gave rise to them, and ultimately how I viewed these narratives. There are these narratives and truths, and then there's my role or choice in it all: my lens on the future, my lens on the past, and my creations in the moment. I made a lot of insights around shifts in society that informed my writing as well.

RC: *What's coming up next?*

YW: I have other book projects that I'm getting out into the world. I really am looking to take some of these books to screen. I'm also creating more experiences in Afrofuturism for people. It's a fascinating time.

28

BOB STEPHENSON
Bit by Bit

Interview by Roy Christopher
Illustration by Laura Persat
May 5, 2018

My favorite actors tend to be those just outside the spotlight. I like character actors and supporting roles. Nicky Katt, Max Perlich, Kevin Corrigan, Steven Weber, Bradley Whitford, Stephen Root, Don McManus, and Daryl Mitchell are some of my favorites.

A little further afield, I'm always paying attention to the background. I love Norman Brenner, who was Michael Richards's stand-in on all nine seasons *Seinfeld* and popped up on camera as an extra in twenty-nine episodes. Ruthie Cohen, who aside from the four main characters, was in more episodes of that show than anyone (101). How about that long-haired guy in the background in damn near every scene of *30 Rock*? Those are the real heroes.

But my absolute favorite is Bob Stephenson. He was the priest-cum-football coach in *Lady Bird* (2017). You might recognize him as the airport security guy in *Fight Club* (1999), but he's been in many other movies and shows you've probably seen: *Felicity, Judging Amy, Without a Trace,* and *Ally McBeal.* In addition to *Fight Club,* he was also in David Fincher's *Se7en*

(1995), *The Game* (1997), and *Zodiac* (2007). He was in both incarnations of *Twin Peaks* (1991/2017). He's been on the current number-one comedy (*Big Bang Theory*) and number-one drama (*NCIS*) in the country. And he was Ted the pilot in the greatest movie of all time, *Con Air* (1997).

Bob also has a deep punk-rock background, but we just talked about filmmaking.

ROY CHRISTOPHER: *How did you get started acting?*

BOB STEPHENSON: I was a production assistant. I did that for about four and a half years. It was really my film school. I always knew I wanted to act, but I didn't want to wait tables. I wanted to be in the thick of it — learn by experience.

RC: *I have often aspired to act in many small roles. I always thought it would be great to have a résumé that read "Guy in Coffee Shop," "Second Cop," "Man #3," and so on. (I was a Papal Emissary on 2 episodes of The Exorcist on Fox and a Bike Messenger in a scene that was cut from an episode of* Empire, *so it's coming slowly.) While your career has definitely surpassed that, do you want the Big Leading Roles?*

BS: Heck yes! Of course I do. I would love that. I write quite a bit, so I often write roles for myself that I'd love to play.

RC: *Prior to your Father Walther character in* Lady Bird, *my favorite of your performances was in* Fight Club. *Both of those roles really display your keen sense of comedic timing and delivery. Do you feel a leaning either toward comedy or drama?*

BS: Comedy for sure. But I like it all.

RC: *You've worked with the best directors doing it, or at least the best Davids (e.g., Fincher and Lynch). Is there someone else you'd most like to work with?*

BS: John C. Reilly.

RC: *You've also written and produced projects yourself. Do you aspire to exact a vision from behind the scenes over being in the scenes?*

BS: Like I said, I write. I love writing and producing. Think I'll leave the directing to someone else (though it would be fun to do that as well).

RC: *What's coming up next?*

BS: About to pitch a TV pilot to studios. Writing another one as we speak. Both comedies.

29

PAT CADIGAN
Eyes on the Skies

Interview by Roy Christopher
Illustration by Eleanor Purcell
April 30, 2018

Widely regarded as one of the original cyberpunks, Pat Cadigan's science-fiction roots run deep. Two of her first three novels won the Arthur C. Clarke Award. She and Robert Heinlein were friends. She's edited sci-fi and fantasy magazines all the way back to the late 1970s. She's been thinking about the future of humans and technology longer than most of us have been around.

In Ted Mooney's novel *Easy Travel to Other Planets* (Farrar, Straus, and Giroux, 1981), he writes,

> the best way to prepare for the future is to keep an eye on the sky. That's where everything else is not. Meanwhile, information pours invisibly across its friendly expanse, and it is up to us to absorb as much of it as our systems can tolerate.

"Cadigan's work makes the invisible visible," Bruce Sterling writes with emphasis. "Certain aspects of contemporary reality emerge that you didn't used to see…" Aptly enough, Sterling and fellow cyberpunk Lewis Shiner both use blades and bleeding to describe her writing. She has a cutting style that could only come from a very sharp mind. She was diagnosed with terminal cancer in 2014, but I'll let her tell you about that.

Though you'd be hard pressed to dig her out of her place in science fiction history, Cadigan has long since been looking up.

ROY CHRISTOPHER: *Given the techno-evangelism of the era in and form which it emerged, cyberpunk provided a cautionary corrective of sorts. Erika M. Anderson, who records under the name EMA, contends that we need cyberpunk's skepticism now more than ever. Others claim we're now living in the world that cyberpunk predicted and that it can no longer help us. Which is it?*

PAT CADIGAN: Damned if I know. I'm still skeptical but then, I've always been skeptical. I didn't realize 2014 was the year cyberpunk broke — was there a memo or a newsletter? If it broke, how did it break?

Cyberpunk was identified as such only after it had been around for a while. The original writers, myself included, didn't sit down and say, "okay, what the world needs now is something called cyberpunk, and here it is." Cyberpunk was a reflection of the larger dissatisfaction and unrest in general, as well as a reaction against the old SF tropes.

I don't disown cyberpunk, I don't distance myself from it, and I'm still writing about things that interest and concern me, which is what I've always done.

RC: *In response to the question, "what happened to cyberpunk?," you told* Vice Magazine *in 2012, "nothing 'happened,' it's just more evenly distributed now."*

PC: I remember saying that to someone, but I don't remember when or why. I've experienced some memory loss since I had chemotherapy — there are things I no longer remember, although I do know I used to remember them, if that makes any sense.

RC: *Well, Cory Doctorow only pointed out that the older cyberpunks talk more slowly than the newer ones.*

PC: The reason for Cory Doctorow's observation is ridiculously easy: older people talk more slowly than younger people because a) we do everything more slowly, and b) we've learned via experience the disadvantage of not thinking twice before we speak. Talking faster doesn't mean you're thinking faster — it just means you're liable to blurt out something you'll have to apologize for afterwards. I've dodged a lot of landmines by talking slowly.

RC: *If we're living in a cyberpunk world, how might we update the genre to help us through it?*

PC: The genre updates itself. I started writing *Synners* in 1988 and finished it in 1990; it was first published in 1991. I wouldn't write that book now — I'm thirty years older, and so is the world. While I often deal with the same general themes, the trappings and details are different.

I've always been an end-user — i.e., I'm not a scientist or a technologist. I don't build machines or write code; I'm the person who always gets the faulty monitor or the computer with the motherboard that shorts out, just like I always got the shopping cart with the wobbly wheel at the supermarket. So these are the things I've written about — how to cope in a world full of faulty equipment and unintended consequences. I'm still writing about that.

RC: *In addition, your stories often play with the relationship between memory and identity. This strikes me as germane given our twenty-first-century media madness. What initially invited you into that conceptual space?*

PC: You would ask me that, wouldn't you? I was always interested in the human brain, for one thing. And for another, when I was growing up, people always seemed to be telling me who I was, or who I was supposed to be. Or they'd assume I was whoever/whatever and expect me to confirm their assumptions, and then get put out when I didn't. Women of my generation weren't supposed to have the same ambitions as men. Men achieved, and we were supposed to help them achieve. There were women who achieved, and there always had been, but in general, they were seen as anomalies. As society saw it, men had ambitions and women had biological clocks.

And those clocks were strictly regulated. As late as 1978, I was unable as a single woman to get maternity insurance along with my regular health insurance through my employer. I had to be married to qualify. When I was growing up, it was standard practice for health insurance companies to refuse to cover the birth of a child out of wedlock or if the woman had a baby before she had been married for nine months, unless her doctor confirmed in writing that the birth was premature.

This probably seems far afield of your original question. But in fact, society has always been trying to tell me who I am. Now I'm a senior citizen, and society is still at it, worse than ever. I went to a cell phone store one day to get some technical help. The salesperson thought I wanted to know how to change the ringtone. It was all I could do not to clobber him with the phone. When my iPad went wonky after an update, I took it to the Apple store after resetting it numerous times didn't work. The man who helped me insisted on walking me through the resetting procedure step-by-step, teaching me as if I had never seen an iPad before.

RC: *Given our internet-driven aggregating and sharing, is all of this cultural recycling really that new?*

PC: It may seem new to some people, but no. In the old days, grasshopper, this was how we made textbooks and schools.

RC: *I've been exploring similar territory in the context of hip-hop (i.e., sampling, nostalgia, etc.), and I'm finding lots of parallels between cyberpunk and hip-hop.*

PC: Well, I can't help you there. I listen to a lot of hip-hop, but I'm only a listener. For the last three-plus years, I've had my hands full with surviving terminal cancer for as long as I can. So far, I'm over a year past my original estimated date of departure. Still not doing what they tell me to.

RC: *Is there anything coming up you'd like to bring up here?*

PC: Just keep watching the skies.

30

MISH BARBER-WAY
Flour Power

Interview by Roy Christopher
Illustration by Laura Persat
July 17, 2017

An energetic and angsty mix of hard rock and post-punk, Vancouver's White Lung sounds like a well-choreographed fist-fight between, say, Girlschool and Fuzzbox. The tense fusion of Mish Barber-Way's vocals and Kenneth William's guitar-work sounds like no other band you've heard, and it makes for downright unforgettable songs. With four records released in six years, White Lung is as prolific as their songs are fast. The latest, *Paradise* (Domino, 2016), is stunningly seductive.

Even so, White Lung is only one arm of Barber-Way's full-frontal haranguing of hegemony. As a Senior Editor at *Penthouse,* Barber-Way writes about things other folks don't dare talk about. The taboo is her regular beat — in print and in song.

ROY CHRISTOPHER: *How did you end up on your current path?*

MISH BARBER-WAY: Here's where I'm at in my path right now: I am sitting at work in my office at *Penthouse*. I am on a tour break. I am not thinking about music. You know how I got to California? Because I was bored in my hometown of Vancouver.

I had hit a ceiling as far as my writing career. Vancouver is a small-town masquerading as a big city. I just decided I was going to move to Los Angeles, and I told everyone I was leaving December 30, so I had to be held accountable. And I did it.

But you mean how did I become a singer in a band? I have been musician and a showboat since I was a child and got to know my id. I would sit in front of the mirror and watch myself shaking my hair around. I had one of those Playskool radios with a microphone attachment. I recorded myself hosting fake radio shows with my best friend. When we got older, we put on plays and imitated Madonna. During my childhood, I was a committed figure skater and dancer. That was my life. Everything. I was very self-disciplined and meticulous. I was extremely competitive and hard on myself. Then, I became a teenager, discovered punk and started learning guitar. I moved out young. I started a band called White Lung with my best friend, Anne-Marie Vassiliou. I finished my university education, but it took me so long because I had to work a few jobs to pay my way. I always liked writing. I knew I wanted to write. I did the thing anyone else does to get what they want: hustled my ass. I worked for free. I did internships and busted my butt at shitty night jobs. I worked hard and tried to learn. Along the way, I found my voice.

RC: *Did you start as more of a writer or a musician?*

MBW: I had been working towards both of these careers equally. The difference is that with music, I never expected to make money from it. I played in a band because I loved making music, and all my friends were in bands, and that was our livelihood, not my bread and butter. When White Lung is writing an album, the lyrics are the most important thing to me. Of course, I want to make great choruses, and melodies, but the lyrics are my main concern. In that sense, I am more of a writer. I want to write a book soon.

RC: *You write about topics most people don't talk about. Do you think that if we talk often, openly, and loudly about sex and drugs, attitudes about them will change?*

MBW: I wrote about those things mostly to keep myself in check. This interview I did explains it well. The confessional style of writing has become the *it* girl. Every girl and their tampon talks about fucking and drugs. It went mainstream with Elizabeth Wurtzel, and it ended with Cat Marnell. I did it because I grew up reading writers and lyricists who wrote like that. I thought it was the only way. I like confessional, bleeding-heart bullshit or heavy, academic research. I like history. Women writers are all the rage right now! Feminism has gone mainstream. Feminism has gone mainstream. I am not entirely interested in identifying myself with this fourth-wave movement, or really with any group. I just want to be treated as an individual. I am a feminist on my terms, not what is the popular rhetoric of millennials. Much of today's online feminism takes no personal responsibility. It demands equality, while asking for special treatment. It calls masculinity "toxic," which I disagree with for many reasons. It blames society, capitalism, and the patriarchy for all women's unhappiness, to which I also I disagree. While there is a lot of power and positivity in current feminism, I also find it fails to see the big picture. The older I get the more I want to live in the country and disappear. The world is way too noisy.

RC: *I recently painted a mural part of which depicted a skateboarding woman. I got shit for the fact that she was white. It struck me as odd that no one commented that it was a woman — not a dude — just that she was white. So, when the revolution comes, will there be a place for white women?*

MBW: What revolution?

You should be allowed to paint whatever ethnicity you want. People are insatiable! They are never satisfied. Look at Mattel, and the Barbie makeover. Women have been complaining about Barbie's impossible portions for decades. So, Mattel buckles under the pressure of the buyers and makes a whole new set of Barbie dolls of all ethnicities, shapes, and sizes, and people still complained. It wasn't enough. We are in a very, very special time in history.

31

CHRIS KRAUS
Wildly Contradictory

Interview by Roy Christopher
Illustration by Laura Persat
June 1, 2017

We have a tendency to want to keep the objects of our admiration in their boxes, like collectors. When one refuses to fit or stay there, we struggle with how to perceive them. It's rare and getting more so, but Chris Kraus is one of those un-box-able entities. Mixing theory, fiction, and biography, her writing confounds as it captivates. She's mostly known for her art writing, but she's also done performance art and film, and she teaches at the European Graduate School.

Through their work with the imprint Semiotext(e), Kraus and her partners, Sylvère Lotringer and Hedi El Kholti, have facilitated works by Jean Baudrillard, The Invisible Committee, Eileen Myles, Kathy Acker, Jarrett Kobek, Franco "Bifo" Berardi, Gilles Deleuze, Félix Guattari, Guy Debord, Julia Kristeva, Gerald Raunig, and Michel Foucault, as well as themselves and many others. As the author Rick Moody puts it, "Semiotext(e) has for a generation been the leading edge of the most incendiary and exciting intellectual revolution in the West."

Kraus's debut novel, *I Love Dick* (Semiotext(e)/Native Agents, 1997), has been adapted into a TV series for Amazon by Jill Soloway and Sarah Gubbins starring Katherine Hahn, Griffin Dunne, and Kevin Bacon. If that weren't enough, her biography of Kathy Acker, *After Kathy Acker* (Semiotext(e)/Native Agents, 2017), is also coming out later this year.

ROY CHRISTOPHER: *For the uninitiated, what would you say your field of work is? Where do you fit?*

CHRIS KRAUS: Writing. Sub-categories — literary fiction; criticism.

RC: *Is having your debut novel turned into a TV show more validating or terrifying?*

CK: Definitely not validating. The real validation came early on, when these girls would show up at bookstore readings with their copies with hundreds of post-its and cracked spines.

It was initially terrifying, but then I realized — who cares? And they're doing a really good job.

RC: *Do you ever feel like a stunt person for your fiction?*

CK: No. More like the director.

RC: *Some of us have the tendency to get ourselves into situations that might make good stories. In another interview, you called infatuation a "gateway drug for writing," which strikes me as a similar, if unplanned, tactic.*

CK: Yeah, the point is that nothing is planned, and what seems like a small incident can become huge. It's all what you read into it.

RC: *You wrote in* Video Green *(Verso, 2004), "I think stupidity is the unwillingness to absorb new information." This sentiment seems all the more germane now.*

CK: Yes, unfortunately so. And there's so much new information, it's almost impossible to absorb.

RC: *I was thinking about that quotation in the context of the current administration, and, more relevantly, the supporters thereof.*

CK: Yes, and that would extend to "ourselves," especially the ones who didn't see it coming.

RC: *Finally, why isn't there already a biography of Kathy Acker? I'm glad you're the one who wrote this one, but doesn't it seem like it should've already happened?*

CK: Yes and no. It takes a long time to research and write a biography. Douglas Martin finished his doctoral dissertation on Acker's work, *When She Does What She Does,* ten years after her death in 2007. Now there's another Acker biography in the works by the Canadian journalist Jason McBride. I think the smoke of Acker's image needed to clear for her work and life to be freshly considered.

RC: *Yeah, there was definitely no box for Kathy Acker.*

CK: No, she was wildly contradictory!

RC: *Do you feel a kinship with her?*

CK: Of course.

RC: *Is there anything else you'd like to bring up here?*

CK: Not yet. But thank you.

32

SIMON CRITCHLEY
The Skull beneath the Skin

Interview by Alfie Bown
Illustration by Roy Christopher
March 9, 2016

Simon Critchley is one of the most well-known and well-respected philosophers alive. His latest text has been read as fiction, as a personal memoir, and as a philosophical essay. In truth, *Notes on Suicide* (Fitzcarraldo Editions, 2015) is all and none of these things. It tells personal stories, his own and those of others, and engages the reader individually, but it retains the philosophical and theoretical rigor of the rest of his life's work. The text is an exploration of Critchley's own relationship to suicide, a discussion of the role of suicide in popular and celebrity culture and a philosophical investigation into the problematic discourses surrounding suicide in contemporary society.

The book is often all of these things at one and the same moment. For example, a central claim that Critchley makes is that "we lack a language for speaking honestly about suicide because we find the topic so hard to think about, at once both deeply unpleasant and gruesomely compelling." With this in mind, suicide notes, to which a chapter is dedicated, are "failed attempts in the sense that the writer is communicating a failure to communicate, expressing the desire to give up in one last attempt at expression." This argument, while making perfect sense on the level of lived experience, also opens out onto a broader philosophical discussion about the limits of language, the proximity of writing to death and the condition of subjectivity as predicated on a fundamental inability to communicate. This move is indicative of the book's unique success in walking a balance between the personal on the one hand and the political and philosophical on the other. Ultimately the book shows that, when it comes to the most important thing, our own lives, the personal and the philosophical are never as separate as it seems.

ALFIE BOWN: *I've found it very interesting how different readers have responded to your book. Some have seen it as personal memoir or even as fiction (possibly because with Memory Theatre, which was out just before, you are writing what can be more clearly defined as fiction), whereas others have not considered that way of thinking about the book at all, reading it as the latest of your philosophical texts. How do you see the book, as fiction, personal memoir, or philosophy?*

SIMON CRITCHLEY: I think it's a combination, but its core is personal and bound up with a difficult situation I've been going through in the last couple of years. I decided to respond to the question of suicide in the only way I can, not directly in a confession but indirectly in writing. In writing we step outside ourselves and many enter a space of death. That's not very cheerful is it?

AB: *One of the things you discuss is the long history of associating suicide with sin and part of your project in this book is to combat this, would that be fair? What should we do about this?*

SC: The first thing we can do is to remove the crazy idea that suicide is a sin. It is not. Neither should suicide be against the law. Assisted suicide should be legalized immediately and the church and the state should just get out of the way. Suicide can sometimes be a failure to the person who kills themselves, but sometimes it is not. My book is an attempt to give us a vocabulary for beginning to talk about suicide like adults and have a proper discussion about the topic. At present, suicide is experienced as a kind of inhibition, and we don't know what to say, apart from the usual banalities.

AB: *Right, so this leads to your argument that we ought to have the right to decide how to live and how to die in a social context that always penalized suicide. We live in a society that both legally and discursively makes suicide into a criminal and sinful act, a breaking of social laws. Suicide is absolutely something that society prohibits. Do you think it should be more of a personal than social issue, something that should be our own personal choice?*

SC: It's a personal issue. It is the most personal issue we can face, whether to live or die. And we have that power in our hands, literally. We can choose to end our lives. But we can also choose to continue to live, which is what I would recommend in the strongest possible terms. The point is that it has to be a choice: to be or not to be. The problem is that that choice is take out of our hands by law, the state, and the church, and I think that's wrong and an abomination. The first part of my book is an attempt to show the basis for the legal prohibition of suicide in Christian theology. Jesus say nothing about suicide, nor does the Hebrew Bible. The prohibition against suicide arises in Catholic theology in the middle ages and that wouldn't matter unless it didn't shape our understanding of law. This is the story I tell in the book. Whether one lives or dies is a question that has to be decided freely by each of us.

AB: *In the book, you use suicide notes as a tool for analysis, treating the suicide note as a unique kind of literary text that needs analysis as much as any other text does, perhaps even more so. I also found it fascinating to read about your workshop on suicide-note writing. Why are suicide notes so important to understanding suicide, and what is their role as objects of study in this debate?*

SC: There is a whole chapter of the book on suicide notes. It's a fascinating topic, but it also lies under a prohibition. We need to be able to see and read suicide notes and understand them as a strange dialectic of exhibitionism and melancholia, of expressions of profound self-hatred, but also as the most sincere declarations of love. They are fascinating documents and modern too. The suicide note, to my knowledge, begins in the eighteenth century in England, and they were usually sent to the press for publication. Suicide notes are attempts at communication, last, desperate attempts to communicate what cannot be communicated. It's grim stuff, but we need to look and to understand.

AB: *One of the things that my own project Everyday Analysis has discussed is death in media culture. While your book isn't so much about popular culture, you do think about the context of the death of artists like Robin Williams, Philip Seymour Hoffman, Kurt Cobain, Hunter S. Thompson, and other icons of mainstream culture. Do you think this kind of fetishism, this bizarre popular race to discuss the dead on Facebook, is a good way or a bad way to help to normalizes suicide and to encourage discussion about it?*

SC: No, this is not a pop essay. But it did begin with the reaction to the deaths of Philip Seymour Hoffman and Robin Williams in New York City. I knew Philip a little and did have a conversation about happiness with him, where we talk about death quite openly. People in NYC were profoundly moved by the death of Philip because he was such a nice man and had fought so long with addiction problems. The reaction to the death of Robin Williams was similar. People were immensely moved. But they didn't know what to say or how to react because our societies still live under the prohibition of suicide. We have to remove the prohibition and begin to speak. It's as simple as that.

AB: *Let me ask you something just outside the remit of the book perhaps. All these examples of suicides that I gave above, and the ones you mentioned, were men. This is an idea that we already have read in feminists and gender studies and is a fact that male* *suicides outnumber female suicides. Do you have an idea about why this might be?*

SC: I did a lot of sociological research for this book, most of which I didn't use in the finished publication. It just didn't fit. One thing I researched but didn't write about was the relation between gender and suicide. Men are three to four more likely to commit suicide than women. The reasons for this might be because of the pressure to be masculine, but that is far from clear from the evidence I have seen. By contrast, three to four as many women as men *attempt* suicide, particularly women in their teenage years and into their 20s. Part of the reason I didn't write about this is that I'm not a sociologist, and it is very questionable to draw inferences from partial data. For example, in China three to four times more women kill themselves than men, often women in conditions of rural poverty, often using pesticides. In general, I think that women have a much more healthy and thoughtful relationship to suicide and death than most men I know.

AB: *I think our readers will be particularly interested in this last question, given what we've been covering at the* Hong Kong Review of Books *lately. One thing we've discussed is the Roy Scranton's book* Learning to Die in the Anthropocene *and the idea that we're all on the way out and all that matters is how we want to go. Do you think all that matters is how we die? Or to put the question a more direct way, is this all pessimistic, or is there some hope?*

SC: Well, I'm still alive, so the book worked for me. [Laughs.] But seriously, I tried to go very deep in this book and really look at the skull beneath the skin. There is a pessimism here, for sure, but for me, as a reader of Nietzsche, this is a pessimism of strength and courage. That's what we need in my view. My book ends with Virginia Woolf's Mrs. Ramsay affirming life: "it is enough," she says, "it is enough." Life is a beautiful thing, but only when we stop being stupidly optimistic and have the courage to look death in the face and maybe even laugh.

33

CLAY TARVER
Gone Glimmering

Interview by Roy Christopher
Illustration by Josh Row
November 7, 2014

I first came across Clay Tarver in the very early 1990s. His guitar playing drove two of my favorite bands back then: Bullet LaVolta and Chavez. The former was, like a lot of the bands of the time, a hybrid of punk, metal, and some third strain of rock that was brewing but had yet to boil. I noticed producer Dave Jerden's name on the back of several CD jackets in and near my player: Red Hot Chili Peppers' *Mother's Milk,* Jane's Addiction's *Nothing's Shocking,* Alice in Chains' *Facelift,* Armored Saint's *Symbol of Salvation,* and Bullet LaVolta's *Swandive. Swandive* (RCA), Bullet LaVolta's last proper record, came out the same day as Nirvana's *Nevermind* (DGC), September 24, 1991. They broke up not long after.

Tarver's next band, Chavez, recorded two of the best records of the decade, both of which sound as firm and fresh now as they did then. *Gone Glimmering* (1995) and *Ride the Fader* (1996) helped Matador Records maintain a hand in the chokehold on the decade-defining sound. (The other hand belonged to Sub Pop.) Along with Matt Sweeney's lilting vocals, it was Tarver's guitar that formed that sound. I've always considered him among players whose guitar sound is their band's identity. Think John Haggerty, Bob Mould, J. Mascis, Steve Albini.

I saw Chavez play in Seattle in 1996, and after the show I went to say "hi" to Clay. I shook his hand and introduced myself, then noticed that I'd interrupted a three-way conversation-in-progress. There were mildly annoyed dudes standing on either side of me. I soon realized I was standing between Greg Dulli and Donal Logue, two of Tarver's old friends and stars in their own right. Dulli is the lead singer of the legendary Afghan Whigs, and Logue, though he's done tons of other things, was the dad on Fox's *Grounded for Life* (2001–5) and currently plays Harvey Bullock on Gotham.

I recently asked Donal about Clay, and he had the following to say:

> Clay Tarver is smarter and more talented than anyone I've ever met, but the super-human thing about Clay is he's never been an attention-seeker or used any of his insanely unfair talents in some kind of narcissistic pursuit. He was the last word in any conversation regarding art or politics, but (and this is hard to articulate), he was never a dick about it. He was always just right, and his thinking was always at another level. High-school, all-state basketball star? I wouldn't have known it unless his family told me. One of the best guitarists of all time? His own kids didn't know he played guitar. No one has influenced me more than Clay Tarver. It's impossible to describe Clay Tarver in a sentence, Roy, so I don't even want to try!

Donal reiterated that the thing he finds so amazing about Clay is his modesty. "What really blows me away," Donal said, "is how he avoided any kind of self-serving behavior, despite his gifts and talents."

Toward the turn of the millennium, Tarver made the switch from music to movies and put together some outstanding and memorable clips in a place where it's difficult to stand out. He directed the "Jimmy the Cabdriver" spots for MTV, which featured

Donal as a greasy, fast-talking cabdriver, directed the ubiquitous "Got Milk?" commercials, and co-wrote the feature film *Joy Ride* (2001) with J.J. Abrams. He now serves as a consulting producer and writer for HBO's *Silicon Valley*. Tarver recently signed on to script the sequel to *Dodgeball* for Fox, but he says that's not likely to happen. He also owes Greg Dulli a phone call.

ROY CHRISTOPHER: *You've been on stage as a guitarist and are now writing scripts and producing. How do the two roles — one out in front of the crowd and one behind the scenes — compare? Which do you like better?*

CLAY TARVER: Well, the first question is easy. Being on stage is one hell of a lot more fun. And not because you're the focus of the attention, of all the applause, etc. To me, it's more about getting some kind of visceral gratification for what I'm doing as it happens. It's tremendous. There's nothing like performing with a group, in front of people, where you're kind of all in this special moment together. Writing is the opposite. Writing is all about creating that moment for others. Sometimes fool-proofing it. It's about craft and discipline and serious self-editing. And I suppose I enjoy the challenge. I do. Even in music, you can't get on stage without doing the hard work of writing. But writing's not fun. Look, I feel very fortunate to be doing what I do. I'm creatively challenged to the hilt. But I'd be lying if I told you I don't miss playing whenever I wanted to.

RC: *Man, the 1990s were a weird time for music. Looking back, it seems like genres were bending and blending in such odd ways. What do you like these days?*

CT: Huh. I don't know if I agree with you. For me, my favorite time of music was the *Creem* magazine days. Genres were all over the place. Any issue could have Cheap Trick, Aerosmith, The Sex Pistols, Blondie, KISS, Nugent, Elton John, Rick Derringer, and Bowie.

The '90s were more a generational thing to me. I was glad to be a part of it. But it was much more sort of straightforward. What am I into today? Not much new. Tinariwen. Queens. Still listening to a lot of Dennis Wilson and Glen Campbell. Love the Master's Apprentices. Saw John Prine for the first time recently and loved it.

RC: *Fair enough... Donal Logue and Greg Dulli are two guys whose paths have crossed yours at various times over the past twenty-odd years. Tell me about the connection among you three.*

CT: Donal was my roommate in college. And he was Bullet LaVolta's road manager and general best friend. He came on tour with us.

In Champaign, Illinois the day of the World Series Earthquake — twenty-five years ago last month — we met and have all been friends ever since. In fact, I owe Greg a call right now (he lives right near me), and he gets real pissy when I owe him one.

Donal and I later did the cab driver things. I'd gotten a job at MTV when I moved to New York City to start Chavez. That's actually how I became a writer. They wanted to turn it into a feature, so I thought I'd give it a try. I figured if I ever wanted to direct more stuff it would be a good skill to have. The movie never got made. But it gave me my career.

It's funny. I never wanted to be a writer. I was one of those guys who, when I finished college, was thrilled to never write another paper again. Now fucking look at me.

RC: *Ha. Speaking of, you're a writer and consulting producer on HBO's* Silicon Valley, *which is hilarious and accurate as far as my experience in start-ups has been. Have you worked in that world at all?*

CT: Nope. Never. But Mike Judge did a million years ago. He's the creator of the show, and a guy I've done feature work with for something like fifteen years. (A great musician, by the way. Sick stand-up bass player. A pro before he got into animation.)

Also, Alec Berg, our show runner, has a brother who worked in that world. Between us we read, did research, went on trips up there. But we also have really serious advisers who help us. We're in the midst of Season 2 right now. Really in the trenches.

RC: *Awesome! I can't wait to see where it goes next. Okay, having been successful in two different areas of entertainment, do you have any advice for those aspiring musicians or writers out there?*

CT: Ya know, people always want to "break in" to music or film or whatever. But I always found that to be a weird phrase. I think you just do what you want and hope people like it. And now, more than ever, that's possible. Music's great because there's no barrier to entry. You have instruments and guys and you just go do it. If people like it, there ya go. Film is obviously more expensive. But, Christ, there's so many different ways to get stuff out there. People make shorts and bits and all kinds of stuff. And if it's good, usually people will find it. I say just keep doing. Keep making stuff. Keep at it.

RC: *I know you're working on* Dodgeball 2, *but what else is coming up?*

CT: I've got some stuff in the works. *Dodgeball 2* doesn't seem like it's going to happen. But I'm hoping to keep at it with *Silicon Valley*. I have some pretty exciting feature things kicking around. And I'm even making a music-based TV show. But in truth, who the hell knows?

34

NICK HARKAWAY
A Dynastic Succession of Trouble

Interview by Roy Christopher
Illustration by Laura Persat
June 26, 2012

I've been away, immersed in Nick Harkaway's intricately constructed yet sprawlingly seductive, second novel, *Angelmaker* (Knopf, 2012; his first is *The Gone-Away World* [Knopf, 2008]). To wrap a genre around this book is to force it into a jacket that doesn't fit. It's noir, it's science fiction, it's steampunk, it's a lot of things, informed by a lot of other things. William Gibson calls it, "the very best sort of odd." "We live in a muddled-together age where the past continues to play out in the present," Harkaway wrote on his site, "with *Angelmaker*, I wanted that sense of the storylines of the past rolling on and on through us to the future, and a dynastic succession of trouble." "Harkaway" isn't Nick's real last name, and his father is also a writer who doesn't use his real name (John le Carré). Even given his own dynastic succession of trouble as such, I'm not sure whom to compare Harkaway to. His writing is more fun than David Mitchell, smarter than Chuck Pahlaniuk, richer than Neal Stephenson, and just plain better put together than most science fiction. He excels at both story and style.

Another Nicholas (Negroponte) wrote in 1995, "machines need to talk easily to one another in order to better serve people." In *Angelmaker,* machines communicating is part of what signals the book's major crisis. To wit, Harkaway recently wrote an updated version, of sorts, of Negroponte's *Being Digital* (Knopf) called *The Blind Giant: Being Human in a Digital World* (John Murray, 2012).

ROY CHRISTOPHER: *Your dad's a writer too. Did he have an influence on your becoming a writer and subsequently on you as a writer?*

NICK HARKAWAY: Not so much an influence as an understanding that it was a possible thing. For most people, writing is a mystery and a career path for lunatics — I still get asked what my day job is. On the other hand, a lot of people think it's a soft touch, which it most assuredly is not, but I knew from very early on that it was both possible and demanding. That's a huge factor in determining whether someone takes the plunge or not, I think — just knowing it's possible. On that score, of course, I'd also already been a scriptwriter, so I knew I could wrestle with a story, turn out work fast, and respond to pretty robust criticism.

As to Angelmaker, no doubt about it. I told my own story, of course, but I also slightly teased my dad. His work, after all, transformed the spy novel from high adventure to Cold War commentary; from dashing Bond to self-despising Leamas. And here I come along and take it back to this heightened romp, more like *Modesty Blaise* or *Billion Dollar Brain* or something. But there are similar roots, too. We both love Conan Doyle, Wodehouse, Dumas…

RC: *I'm almost finished with* Angelmaker *and am only hoping it doesn't become a movie because I don't want my head's version tampered with. How has your screenwriting experience influenced your novels?*

NH: I see things in my mind's eye very clearly. Not always, but I can't write action sequences without being a little specific. At the same time, I know that everyone wants to imagine them flowing the way they do on the best movies, so you can't explain the mechanics of Ippon Seio Nage, say, while you're having the fight. At the same time, it needs to feel as if you just did. It's sleight of hand, all of it.

And I suppose I have a tendency to use movie shapes, like the Classic Myth Structure George Lucas used for *Star Wars,* because they're dramatic and recognizable, and they keep you on track. Writing the kind of books I write, with lots going on, you need not to get lost. Structure helps. A story spine is vital. And so is knowing what the voice is, the tone. With those, you can go all over the map and come home safe, and you know it, and your reader gets that confidence in you and settles, so you can take liberties and amaze them. The less secure they are, the less likely they are to go with you when you do something unusual; and that unusual thing is often why you're there, so that's bad. They close the book. And once they do that, you have a hell of a time getting them to open it again.

RC: *You mentioned before that you and William Gibson approach writing in different ways. As a writer and one interested in other writer's processes, I wonder if you could elaborate on this.*

NH: Gibson has a little piece about how he writes at the beginning of *Distrust That Particular Flavor* (Putnam Adult, 2012), and it's amazing. It's incredibly him. He starts with a sentence, out of nowhere. To me, that's the hardest thing you can possibly do. To sit there and carve out a piece of writing from nothing, using a beginning to leverage a world inside your head. So here we go:

> Abernathy, like a church mouse, craved simplicity and the smell of wood polish above all things; the intrusion of these men, these police men, into his world was like the arrival of a visiting bishop's cat.

Here's the thing: that sentence has enough tone to turn into a story. There's a world buried in there but it is wedged and cracked and fuzzy and difficult. I'm quite tempted by it, but it would be an uphill struggle to bring it out. And it can go wrong. You can go down a blind alley and find that you're just wrong about everything and you have to start again. The Coen Brothers once said that the best writing comes when you write yourself into a corner and then write out again, and you can see that in their stuff: sometimes they do, and you can't believe your luck, sometimes they don't, and you think "oh, ouch!" I do not like that feeling when it applies to my own work. It makes me feel sad for weeks. I like having a strong sense of the story before I start writing — not a roadmap, but a vibe. Like: "we're going to Canada!" Okay, cool. Now let's start the car.

I tend to start with a blinding image or a concept. An idea hits me, and it has crackling energy all around it, tensions and balances made in. Basically it's a fizzing bomb. And then I crank the beginning up and up and up so that it can support this fizzing thing, and the story is basically the position of items so that when the idea explodes they all fly along the right sort of paths and in the right direction.

I will admit, in honesty, that right now I'm incredibly drawn to Abernathy. I will have to try this kind of approach one day soon. I can see in him the beginning of that kind of bomb, but it feels like doing the whole thing in reverse, in the mirror. And you can already see that my instinct is to place him in conflict immediately, in media res, to flag that possibility of cat and mouse pursuit, and so on. I am, or I have been, so far a busy writer — not that I always produce busy writing — but Gibson has this incredible feeling of restraint, of time enough in the world. Which is deceptive, because he can wallop you with tension and pace whenever he wants. He's that guy from all the martial arts movies with the wispy hair who sits all day long in stillness — and then you try to pour a glass of water on his head, and you can't because somehow he already drank it, and now he's holding your shoes. I'm more like a conjuror. I stack the deck.

RC: *I can relate. I never start from a blank page. Whom else do you enjoy reading?*

NH: Oooooh, so many people. I just read Robin Sloan's fabulous *Mr. Penumbra's 24 Hour Bookstore* (Farrar, Straus, and Giroux, 2012), and Ned Beauman's *The Teleportation Accident* (Bloomsbury, 2013). I got sent early copies of both, by editors with great judgement for what I'm going to like, but I love all kinds of things. Jeanette Winterson and Don DeLillo, Lois Mc Master Bujold and Rex Stout. I just finished John Scalzi's *Redshirts* (Tor, 2012), and I thought it was stunningly good. It made me cry at the end, although that's not hard because I'm basically a wuss. But if you want to see something interesting, examine *Redshirts* alongside *Teleportation Accident*. There's a really interesting structural mirroring which I think comes from which of them is writing for which audience, but they're closing on one another in this really intriguing way.

RC: *You're primarily known as a novelist, so how did* The Blind Giant *come about?*

NH: The short version is that the John Murray imprint came to me and asked me to do it, and I wanted to. The slightly longer answer is that in the UK I was one of the first and loudest objectors to the Google Book Settlement, which I thought took a brilliant idea (a global digital library) and saddled it with the wrong method (a private company making an end run around the legislative process — consider that in the context of, say, BP), and the wrong endgame (a private company being the only entity with the right to display some books and becoming the de facto library of record). From that I ended up talking about digital books and the broader issues of digitization a lot, and here we are. Well, no, that's not quite true. I've always been a student of politics and society, and their relationship with science, technology, and the individual.

RC: *Tell me about the book. I'm avoiding reading it right now as I fear it may out-mode my current book-in-progress.*

NH: Oh, yes, I know that feeling. I'm binge-reading right now because I'm between books. Well, okay, *The Blind Giant* is broad by design. That's to say that it tries not to get into drilldown about specific issues, or to "solve" them, but to look at where each issue folds into the next and how they all relate to one another. I realized after finishing the book that the whole discussion is framed in my mind partly as a conflict between our intentional actions and the emergent ones which come from our collective and somewhat undirected or unconsidered choices. We have a chance for the first time to begin to understand, in real time, what world we're making and how even to change the direction of that making. That's superb. (Hence the title: imagine for a moment that all your sense data arrived five or ten minutes late. You'd constantly be falling over, misunderstanding conversations, and breaking things. Our body politic has had a delay of ten to fifty years until very recently. No wonder it keeps getting into fights and staggering around like a drunken sailor.)

So, the book embraces a little bit of recent history, an overview of the last hundred years, a discussion of deindividuation — the process by which ordinary people can do appalling things to one another, as seen in the notorious Stanford Prison Experiment — some stuff of the science of the brain and the sociology of the digital environment, the politics of us, the connection between copyright and privacy, the jurisprudence of intellectual property. It goes where the digital debate goes, because the thing about digital is that it's our reflection. It's not separate. It's neither especially good nor especially pernicious. It's us. And I didn't try to crush opposing positions. The book has some footnotes, but they're not like "nyah nyah, you are broken on my genius" footnotes, they're like "this is where I got this idea from, okay?" So, it's a digital book in that sense too: it takes an iterative approach to the right answer — fail, get closer, fail, get closer. Although whether there'll ever be a revised edition…

who knows? The idea was that the iterations would be conversations arising from the text, persisting in the public sphere rather than falling back to paper. Because, you know, less work for me.

RC: *What are you working on next?*

NH: I have a first draft of a new novel. I'm calling it "Tigerman Make Famous Victory, Full of Win," and I can already feel my editors wincing and wondering how to persuade me that's an appalling title, but I'm really determined about it. It's about a guy on an island that is about to be destroyed to contain a chemical waste problem. As a consequence, the island has become Casablanca-ish. It's a bit different from my first two. After that I have this thriller burning a hole in my pocket, and then there's my story about cryonics and the other one about cricket and another one about a six thousand year old child. Oh, and there's one which is basically a crime novel about tortoises which is also about the publishing industry — and let's just say I have a lot of work to do.

35

SIMON REYNOLDS
Erase and Start It Again

Interview by Alex Burns and Roy Christopher
Illustration by Josh Row
September 17, 2007

Simon Reynolds writes about music like a cross between a diehard fan and an open-headed academic, sitting him decidedly on the fence between the pit and the podium. From this spot, he's able to write both enthusiastically and critically. His books, *Bring the Noise* (faber & faber, 2007), *Rip It Up and Start Again: Postpunk 1978–1984* (Penguin, 2006), and *Generation Ecstasy: Into the World of Techno and Rave Culture* (Routledge, 1999), cover the major movements of the of underground music over the past thirty years and provide a crash course in the underpinnings of today's mix of repurposed technology and styles, recycled beats and sounds, and the attitudes and energy driving it all.

Fellow traveler and *Disinformation* editor Alex Burns joined me in asking Simon a few questions about his books, his writing, and what's coming up next.

ALEX BURNS: *What prompted you to make the rise-fall arc of John Lydon and Public Image Ltd's "careering" central to* Rip It Up And Start Again? *What lessons could emerging artists learn from how*

PiL handled its contract negotiations with Virgin Records and the "fault lines" between Lydon, Jah Wobble, and Keith Levene?

SIMON REYNOLDS: PiL were probably my favorite postpunk band, certainly the one that had the most impact on me. But beyond the personal inclination, it just seemed to be objectively the key narrative in terms of explaining how punk turned into postpunk, and then how postpunk eventually fell into disarray. You had the central figure of the era, Johnny Rotten, the punk savior, the man everyone was looking toward, completely confounding expectations and going on this total art trip with PiL. You had all the incredibly influential rhetoric that Lydon, Wobble, and Levene put out there about rock being dead and "obsolete," rock as something that should be "cancelled," "a disease" is one word they used to describe it. And PiL's diagnosis of punk's failure on a musical level, that it had been the last gasp of traditional rock. A lot of people followed Lydon's lead. But the saga of how it all went wrong for PiL is classic, because the irony is that this band opposed to all things "rock" was undone by all the archetypal rock'n'roll bullshit of drugs, ego, money disputes, mismanagement. They didn't have management, basically. Indeed they could probably have used a proper manager, but Lydon had been scared off that because of his experiences with Malcolm McLaren. It would make a great VH1 *Behind the Music* story, actually. They also came unstuck in a way that was emblematic of postpunk in general, which is reaching a kind of dead end with experimentation and deconstruction, with their third album *Flowers of Romance*. That came out just at the point at which postpunk turned to new pop, the more optimistic and accessible music of Orange Juice, ABC, etc., etc.

In terms of the contract, I'm not sure they actually had that great arrangement with Virgin. A manager would have been handy in that respect. I think they were indulged by Virgin, given lots of studio time, but then again Virgin probably charged them for using the Manor and the other top of the line studios. Virgin supported Lydon because they could see he was obviously the most important front man to come out of Britain since

Bowie. But they also tried to persuade him to reform the Pistols at one point. Branson played him the demos by the Professionals, the band that Paul Cook and Steve Jones formed, and said "isn't this great Johnny? How about reforming the band?" There was a hope that he would revert to doing more accessible music and become a superstar. Which is what Lydon actually tried to do eventually, but still under the PiL brand.

AB: *You wrote about the "dark side of paranoid psychology," "totalitarian undercurrent," and "music as a means to an end" of Throbbing Gristle and Genesis P-Orridge's first mission. How significant is Throbbing Gristle's re-emergence, and what new alienations could this new mission evoke?*

SR: I'm not sure what it signifies beyond the fact that the band members felt like doing it and that at this point in history the climate for them doing that is more welcoming than it has been for a while. Also, they are probably keen to reaffirm their place in history, which is totally understandable. I was a bit surprised how little impact their return to the scene had. I thought it would be a much bigger deal, if only because it's such a great story for magazines. But I guess this sometimes happens, especially when a band has been so groundbreaking, they suffer a little bit when they return to a music world that they've changed. Because everyone's like, big deal. I thought the album was really good myself.

AB: *Your analysis of music and political subcultures highlights a "lifecycle" (i.e., experimentation, discovery, a golden or "heroic" age, entropy, and reemergence or revival). What can other analysts and critics learn from this approach? What are the possibilities and limits of a "lifecycle" model?*

SR: It's hardly an original way of looking at cultural movements! But if it is a cliché, it's one of those "cliché-because-it's-true" situations, I think. In my experience, music genres or scenes seem to coalesce out this longish period of germination, disparate things gradually come together; there's some kind of spark or flash-over moment when it all converges and reaches fruition, the momentum gets going, the sound evolves and quite quickly reaches maturity; after this "prime" period, things start disintegrating, the center will not hold, all kinds of tangents and offshoot genres split away while a purist faction try to freeze the sound at what they consider is the golden moment. All the energy ebbs away leaving a lot of people feeling disillusioned and burned 'cause they believed so fiercely in it. Then the sound or scene is filed away in the archives where it might be excavated by some future generation.

In some ways the emergent phase in the most interesting phase because often, what's going on around the proto-scene is a period of general disparateness and entropy, no clear direction in music culture. And those periods often are actually quite rich, especially when you look back at them with hindsight, and you wonder what the people trying to launch the new thing were complaining about! Like with punk, it took about five years to get off the ground, and people like Lester Bangs were using the term "punk" to signify the need for some kind of pomposity-removing revolution, and the people reclaiming rock from the bloated superstar elite. He was doing that from about 1970 onwards. There were various false starts, like with the Stooges, or pub rock in the UK. Then finally it all takes off with Patti Smith, Ramones, then the Pistols and Clash. But you look at the early-'70s music scene that they were so fed up with, and it seems, compared to now, jam-packed with exciting things. All quite disparate maybe, but still: what on earth were they so depressed for? But it's also interesting to look at the emergent phase of the movement-to-be, all the lost bands like the Electric Eels in Cleveland, proto-punk outfits here there and everywhere that are isolated and at odds with the general tenor of things, bands that could either be ahead of their time or behind-of-their-time, it's not at all clear. And gradually they all find each other, and BOOM!

ROY CHRISTOPHER: *Your brand of para-academia puts you on the fence between journalist and scholar. Do you find this vantage point to be more of a boon or a burden?*

SR: I can't write from any other place! Well, that's not quite true. I can and have done more standard, music writing. I do quite a lot of fairly straightforward record reviewing, and have in the past done newspaper-type profiles and reporting, still do it now and then. But the mode that I naturally fall into, if left to my own devices, is somewhere between theory and journalism. I find it a good place to be in terms of the work produced, because pure academic work doesn't have much place for enthusiasm, or for a flamboyant prose style. And there's all that slog to do with footnotes and talking about your methodology and your theoretical framework, all that protocol. Academic work on music also suffers from its slow turnaround, and it always seems to be dealing with stuff that's from years and years ago. I like the rapid-response nature of journalism. On the other hand, I like to have an extra dimension or two to work with than just the basic, consumer-guidance level of responding to a record or profiling a band. Larger resonances to do with society or culture beyond music.

So, I would say definitely it's a boon in terms of the work produced, as discrete pieces of writing. In terms of work on the macro level of a career, I think the scope for doing this kind of theory-informed music writing has definitely shrunk significantly. Theory is much less of a cool or sexy thing than it was in the 1980s when I started. But it's also to do with shrinking space, smaller word counts, and the decline of spaces like the alternative weekly in the States and the weekly music press in Britain. Those were havens for pretentious music writing, but, with the exceptions of art magazines and places like the *Wire*, most music magazines and newspapers now seem to have an orientation toward the layperson. You can't assume too much esoteric knowledge of music. But above all, it's the shrinking of space that's key. If a review or piece is being pared to essentials, the first thing that goes is the extraneous theory, the references to thinkers outside the world of pop music.

Personally I haven't felt this as a source of anguish that much, because I've gradually lost interest in doing the critical-theory-infused approach due to not finding much in that world very exciting in the last ten years or so. There was a time when going into St. Mark's Books in downtown New York City, or its London equivalents like Compendium, would get my pulse racing with excitement. But not for a long while. So you won't find too many name-drops of philosophers in my writing these days. I still have my favorites, but they're old ones, and for whatever reason they seem to have less applicability to the music I like. I also feel like I've reached the point where I'm on my own trip, as a thinker about music. I don't need to fuel up on other bodies of thought so much.

RC: *What are you working on next?*

SR: I just finished an expanded/updated version of *Energy Flash*, a.k.a. Generation Ecstasy, with stuff on the last decade of electronic dance culture, and that is due out in early 2008, timed for the tenth anniversary of the book and the twentieth anniversary of rave. Right now, I'm about to embark on the companion volume to *Rip It Up and Start Again*, which will include interview transcripts, essays, and a discography-with-commentary dealing with all the esoteric postpunk music I couldn't cover in the original book. That should be out in 2009. I'm also drawing up plans for my next book proper, but for now I'll have to keep that under wraps.

36

MALCOLM GLADWELL
Epidemic Proportions

Interview by Roy Christopher
Illustration by Eleanor Purcell
November 12, 2002

Malcolm Gladwell's applied epidemiology picks up where the overwrought meme metaphor breaks down. In *The Tipping Point: How Little Things Can Make a Big Difference* (Little, Brown and Co., 2000), Gladwell explores and explains complex social and market phenomena through a sturdy, methodical framework and with engaging, easy-to-understand language. Unlike many social theorists, Gladwell eschews grandiose postulating and sticks to observation and acutely intuitive pattern-recognition.

An ace journalist with an intellect to match, Malcolm Gladwell could just be one of today's most important writers.

ROY CHRISTOPHER: *Can you give potential readers brief overview of what* The Tipping Point *is about?*

MALCOLM GLADWELL: *The Tipping Point* is an attempt to use the principles of epidemiology — the study of epidemics — to understand the movement of ideas and information. I argue that if we want to understand why ideas can be so contagious, and spread so rapidly, we need to think of them as viruses.

RC: *Have you attempted to use your theories to spread themselves?*

MG: Yes! Very early on, before my book came out, my publisher and I spent several weeks, touring around the country, meeting with "book mavens" who we felt could best spread the "tipping point" virus. It's hard to say, but I think it worked!

RC: *Your book manages to brush shoulders with several other theoretical monsters (chaos theory, memetics, etc.) without stepping on any of their toes. Given your subject matter, why did you intentionally avoid talking about the idea of memes in this book?*

MG: Well, I didn't talk about chaos theory, because I felt that Jim Gleick's book on chaos was so brilliant that there was no way I could top it. As for memetics, I hate that theory. I find it very unsatisfying. That idea says that ideas are like genes — that they seek to replicate themselves. But that is a dry and narrow way of looking at the spread of ideas. I prefer my idea because it captures the full social dimension of how something spreads. Epidemiologists are, after all, only partially interested in the agent being spread. They are more interested in how the agent is being spread, and who's doing the spreading. They are fundamentally interested in the social dimension of contagion, and that social dimension, which I think is so critical, is exactly what memetics lacks.

RC: *You mention these ideas in the book and on PBS's* The Merchants of Cool. *Do you think today's youth marketing leaves room for the youth to develop their own culture? Is there time between inception and market for youth culture to grow?*

MG: Oh sure. I think that the one thing that teenagers are very good at doing is building their own, indigenous culture. Teens are so naturally and beautifully social and so curious and inventive and independent that I don't think even the most pervasive marketing culture on earth could ever co-opt them.

RC: *Who do you admire writing about social phenomena these days?*

MG: At the moment, I'm very much fascinated by the latest wave of social psychologists who write about the unconscious: Timothy Wilson, John Bargh, and Mazarin Banarji, among others.

RC: *Are you working on any upcoming projects you'd like to tell us about?*

MG: I'm in the middle of a book about intuition. Stay tuned!

37

WILLIAM GIBSON
The Co-evolution of Humans and Machines

Interview by Kodwo Eshun
Illustration by Roy Christopher
November 1996

KODWO ESHUN: *You're an American writer. How did you come to live here in Shaughnessy, this quaint suburb of Vancouver?*

WILLIAM GIBSON: This isn't really a suburb anymore in North American terms. The real suburbs are past the airport; the suburbs that people commute to everyday, that make the traffic go way, way out there. I go to London or Berlin more frequently than I go out there. This is a 1920s suburb that was built for the first wave of automobiles. When you go that way toward town, where we used to live was actually a 1900 suburb that was pre-automobile, tramway and people would travel from downtown. So it's just layers and layers. There's not really a center there. It's only there because it's surrounded by concentric circles of things that aren't there. Everything moves in. This is still cloyingly middle class, although most of the neighbors are from Hong Kong and Singapore now, which is very funny considering the visuals. If we go out to the park you can sort of see the colonization of it, so it kind of goes mock Tudor, and then these strange, [splutters in amusement] -looking new houses that are built for people from Hong Kong who don't want thatched roofs. They don't like things with wooden roofs. They want concrete tiles.

KE: *I think the way Ballard stayed true to the suburbs was a really inspiring thing. For so long writers would head away from the suburbs and move into London. Ballard was the first writer to say things like, to grow up in the suburbs you have to commit a criminal act everyday in your own mind. Even if you don't actually kick the dog, you have to think about kicking the dog. You have to think about breaking the glass.*

WG: The suburbs are much more dangerous because in the city someone might come up and take your money, but in the suburbs they'll take your soul.

KE: *There's this feeling that you have to assert yourself against this mind-numbing inertia. Once you get into London or Munich or Vancouver you realize that almost everyone is from one kind of suburb or another. Hardly anyone in London comes from there. The center is filled by people malformed by early years of exclusion which drive them on. Maybe growing up at the center of things is one of the worst things that can happen to you. Everything's completed before you've begun.*

WG: Yeah, well, this was like a straight colonial operation. It was part of the British Empire. It was a goofily loyal, little colony, way more so than Australia could ever have been. There was no attitude. These people were just, like, completely patriotic.

KE: *A consensual hallucination-delusion that gripped people.*

WG: I think it was real. At some point it must have been real. When I first came to Canada in the late '60s it was much more evident. It was part of the Commonwealth. The postboxes were red and had the Queen's picture. The Queen was much more prevalent. Today she's just left on the money, but she isn't on the postal vans and police badges. Even in the late '60s, there she was. Excuse me. [Gets up and walks to back door.] Think I've got my wife locked out. [Returns to the desktop with a Powerbook, which we're sitting by. A fax croons in the corner. There's a Robert Longo drawing of guns on the left wall of the rectangular, basement studio.] It was very obviously a colony and that's faded out in the past twenty years. I almost miss it in a way. There was something so peculiar about it. They don't have the graphics design to replace it. All of the official Canadian seals look amateurish.

KE: *That's new. The new always looks shoddy compared to the good old stuff. Let me say how much I enjoyed the new novel* Idoru.

WG: Thank you.

KE: *There's an almost pathological hyperawareness paid to the commodity throughout* Idoru.

WG: Absolutely. You have that in London to an almost equal extent. There are people in London who know more about American menswear than anyone in the United States. I don't often make pronouncements about the real future, but the scariest thing that's happening now is Tommy Hilfiger because that is a simulacrum of a simulacrum and that may be the future.

KE: *A meta-simulacrum.*

WG: Yeah. Ralph Lauren is a simulacrum of Brookes Brothers, and Tommy Hilfiger is a simulacrum of Ralph Lauren. But he's already more ubiquitous than Ralph Lauren ever was. Maybe in the future there will only be one brand and he'll design everything.

KE: *Leading on from Hilfiger's one global brand you have media executive Kathy Torrance's riff in* Idoru *which suggests that we are a shopping species.*

WG: *I do get a certain amount of criticism particularly in America for being too conscious of fashion.*

KE: But it's crucial to start at the surface. Skin is deep.

WG: *Critics get very, very upset that the characters in my books notice what other people are wearing and know what they're wearing themselves. They're soulless. All they can think about is clothes and make up.*

KE: As opposed to?

WG: *I don't know. Beethoven?*

KE: The Proletariat?

WG: *[Laughs.] There's a very peculiar world of literature that doesn't exist which you can infer from criticism and sometimes when I've read twenty reviews of a book I've written, there'll be this kind of ghost book suggested.*

KE: [Laughs.]

WG: *And I wonder about that book, what is that book they would have wanted, and it's a book with no surfaces. [Laughs.] It's all essence.*

KE: From the beginning you've deliberately undated your fiction so there's a powerful sense of time undefined, of time derealized. This produces a chrono-flux, a writing without handrails, without the dates and calendars so much science fiction anchors itself with.

WG: *Actually I was quite upset when my American publishers dated* Virtual Light *on the book's fly-leaf. It's possible to work out a date from internal evidence, but it takes a bit of thought. I suppose I've always wanted to have a hedge against the literal as-*

sumption that these stories are fictions about "the future" rather than attempts to explore an increasingly science fictional present. I think we tend to live as though the world was the way it was a decade ago, and, when we connect with the genuinely contemporary, we experience a species of vertigo.

KE: *You frequently magnify the grain of material. In* Idoru, *Kathy Torrance's shoes have vibram cleats and so do the homicide cops in* Virtual Light. *Simultaneously you drastically demagnify world historical events. By the time of* Idoru, *the US President is an African American woman, but this is revealed with such indifference it's impossible to know what attitude to assume. Maybe the American critics who chastise you for taking fashion too seriously are in fact irritated by your ongoing reversal of the order of things?*

WG: I think of magnification as mimetic; most people, most of the time, are more aware of the fine grain than of world history. But the fine grain is always revealing, and none of the details are random. Both those examples of vibram soles are about recontextualization, for instance. I think a certain kind of critic, usually American, usually male, is simply uncomfortable with the socially descriptive use of the language of fashion. But if it was good enough for Jane Austen, it's good enough for me.

KE: *As soon as you start writing about women, you have scales of surface depth. You access these giant cosmetic industries, which are simultaneously intimate industries. The distance between each eyelash represents the work of countless scientists toiling away in cosmetic labs. You can switch scale very fast between close ups on lipstick and their manufacture. Most women move between the intimate and synthetic in a way that men are completely incapable of. And when you switch from a teenage girl to older women, that's another parameter you can add in.*

WG: Women have the future applied to them constantly.

KE: *Exactly.*

WG: That's a very, very good point. I can get a better science-fiction buzz from a copy of *Vogue* than I can from *New Scientist*. Always! [Laughs.] This has always been true. One of the great science fiction moves of the last decade or so is Bruce Sterling's investigation of the fashion world in *Holy Fire*, his new book. It's brilliant. This twenty-first-century supermodel scene in Europe he's describing is just so funny.

KE: *Fashion is extremely crucial. In the '50s, McLuhan referred to women as mechanical brides, and there's always this feeling if you look at models: there's a certain kind of robotic chic as they take to the runway or the catwalk. There's the whole agonistics of the catwalk: real women can't wear these clothes.*

Of course the real woman is a complete optical illusion. There are no real women. The catwalk is like a laboratory for synthesising new, possible states of womanhood at any one time. The designers are very much like scientists. They're often gay, they're quite cold, and often you can't quite gauge their attitude to women at all. You can't work out whether they really hate them, or whether they really love them. Women, models, are material for the clothes. That often explains women's unease towards designers because women grasp quite clearly that they are material for designers to synthesize. And the women who love fashion understand this and are completely at home with this, and women who don't are made entirely uneasy by the idea that their current state is nothing but material for a future state. When you go to a fashion show you're watching a series of parallel possibilities of what women might turn out like literally: next season you're going to look like this.

WG: That's very interesting. No one's ever pointed out that before.

KE: *The hypermedia economy that your novels describe is incredibly powerful, able to suck in willing subjects and effortlessly spit them out. How did this media ecology emerge?*

WG: Questions like this one presuppose that the books have a substructure, some kind of formal Future History. They don't. Their ecology of media is simply the result of squinting at contemporary media in a particular way. Or, more systematically, of trying to imagine how media would behave if all social brakes were removed. Given the tenor of American television today, this is really fairly easy to do. I think Burroughs had wonderful insights into the more malevolent possibilities of television that's something I notice now in *Naked Lunch*. The sense of television that emerges from *Naked Lunch* is the dark side of network TV that I think is disappearing.

KE: *What is the dark side of network TV?*

WG: Probably that it's hierarchic, it's top down, and it comes to you from a boardroom, its broadcast.

KE: *In terms of hypermediation you've got Kathy Torrance of Slitscan who has this view of her audience as this hungry, amorphous organism, which is eager for ritual bloodletting, which she sees as the alchemical blood of celebrity. How much are you interested in the media performing these kinds of rituals?*

WG: I think in the United States we are very naive about that and it's changing. When we got tabloids, it was television. In England it's been taken for granted for a while, that sort of ritual behavior, but I still find it a bit shocking. Tabloid TV gives me the creeps. That's the American in me. It's fascinating to see what these people are doing. Slitscan is extrapolated from American tabloid TV more than anything else. There's a really interesting sense in the States that the old networks are dying. NBC and CBS can't keep up and there's so much cable. The world of *Idoru* is the eight-hundred-channel universe. They've figured out how to fill them up. There are so many channels, it gets hypersurreal just in an attempt to fill up space.

KE: *These processes like broadcasting, repetition, amplification. Today you get a sense of these as runaway processes that corporations can't control as totally as they'd like to. Like Marinetti and McLuhan, Burroughs was a great media theorist. The tape recorder must have been his parallel to the handheld camera. He had a real insight into the secret life of machines.*

WG: He called it God's Little Toy.

KE: *I think that was Gysin's description.*

WG: Yeah, yeah, Gysin.

KE: *No it wasn't, it was Bowles. I think he saw the tape recorder as the first machine that could deprogram the routines already running you, the metaprograms of the reality studio.*

WG: The tape recorder was the first widely available instrument that allows you to manipulate media. I remember I bought the first Walkman I ever saw. There was one in a shop, and I said what's that, and this guy told me, and I said I'll buy that. I didn't even have a tape recorder. I had to go and get someone to make me a tape. The experience of taking the music of your choice and being able to move it through the environment of your choice had just never been available. It felt weirdly subversive. I could walk through rush-hour crowds listening to Joy Division at skull-shattering volumes [laughs], and no one knew. Like you were having this completely different experience that was completely altering the way it all looked and no one knew.

KE: *You had this sense of public secrecy and secret publicity, which has become ubiquitous. As soon as you had tape recorders you could play with time. Tape recorders made time plastic. In* The Ticket That Exploded, *the tape recorder is a medium that enables you to hear the social machines that are already processing you. I hear the sampler as the third stage in the process where the urban environment becomes a potential ecology of instruments. Sam-*

pling completely destroys the history of causation. You can't locate what you're listening to, so sound and time goes AWOL. *You're abducted by audio, snatched by sound.*

WG: I don't know whether I heard about sampling or whether I invented it for the specific passages in *Neuromancer*. The idea is that the dreads in *Neuromancer* are sampling everything that they've sucked in the whole musical universe, and they're constantly creating this one music as a kind of religious act. In those early books the most intriguing effects came from juxtaposing things I scarcely understood at all. The result could be quite amazing, but in terms of there having been an intellectual structure, often there's nothing at all. The idea of sampling would have been utterly alien and incomprehensible in the '60s.

KE: *The sampler is the instrument that makes other instruments. It's a machine, which makes other machines. It's not a sound source in itself. The sampler doesn't sound like anything. It just feeds in any input and turns that into parameters and envelopes, which can become any sound at all. It has this utopian possibility of being an eternal instrument-making machine.*

WG: Perpetually new.

KE: *Today, people are at home inside machinic processes. Nobody thinks of machines as vampiric processes that will drain your precious life fluid or alienate you from your real self like they did back in the '60s and '70s. The sense today is that technologies are both inhuman and energising. Before the '60s, there was sensory deprivation on a mass scale. In fact to be cultured was to be sensually deprived. Culture meant the negation of the senses at all levels.*

WG: I never think about challenging the machine. It never occurs to me. I mean, Machines R US. These people all think machinery is something from Japan that they get out of a box and they can take it back to the store if it gets on them. The thing is, it not only gets on them it gets under their skin and into their gene structure. We're not at all natural. We're sort of quasi-machines anyway at this point.

KE: *Your critics miss the mix of ecstasy and dread in your work.*

WG: Some guy sitting around wool-gathering [laughs] about "the machines are taking over, the machines are taking over" seems to me to be an utterly pathetic attitude to have this late in the century. Does this guy want all his fillings pulled and his vaccinations reversed? That's machinery too, you know. They took over about 1942 and there's no going back. If we do go back we're going to go back twenty-five years if we're lucky, not having any teeth when we die and eating roots and stuff. I don't think there's any compromise.

KE: *In* Idoru, *Laney's bad drug has stimulated this Attention Deficit Disorder that allows him to drift between nodal points in the mediascape. What would have been denounced back in the twentieth century as channel-zapping, as a debilitating personality flaw, instead turns out to announce a new order of digital perception, of data divination. How did this reversal, this convergence of technological intuition occur to you?*

WG: Well after the fact I came to the conclusion that I was unconsciously trying to figure out what it is I do. I think I'm drifting around looking for nodal points. I identify totally with Laney's frustration at having to try to explain how he does the thing he does to make a living. But I basically do the same thing: I put myself in the way of huge floes of information, none of it terribly interesting or important in itself, and look for the points at which I somehow feel change is about to emerge.

KE: *It's called "information dowsing" as well, isn't it.*

WG: Yeah, yeah. Nodal points are what make foolish people think I'm prescient. In retrospect, I think I was looking for a metaphor for whatever it is that I do that people mistake for a predictive capacity. Also, I think Laney's talent is an "art" thing, and I treasure the nonrational in art.

KE: *There are many sections in* Idoru *where it's all girl action, no guys at all. Still striking compared to traditional science fiction. Your girl and woman characters don't articulate cyber-feminism; they're restless, heedless, and impatient.*

WG: I think of them as being post-feminist in a way. They take a lot of things for granted so much so that they're not consciously politicized. They just seemed to have emerged from somewhere where they have several more degrees of freedom. They don't have to think about it anymore. The thing that scares me most about prison is not being locked up, it's being in there with nothing but guys. Science fiction had been this all-male environment. I was very lucky when I started writing in the late-'70s and early-'80s because the most interesting thing that was happening in science fiction in the US was a very, very intense feminist tendency that was centered in Seattle and Portland. Joanna Russ was in Seattle and Ursula Le Guin was in Portland.

KE: *Women are just so used to synthesising and manufacturing themselves. As soon as you look at makeup in magnification, it becomes fascinating. A friend showed me this history of makeup in the twentieth century, the key dates when eyeliner, when lipstick was first produced, and as you looked you realized you were looking at the consolidation of the woman machine. We know so much about the man machine, but, through cosmetics, there's this woman machine slowly emerging from the laboratories. People think of labs as centers for geneticists and rocket scientists, but labs are where cosmetics come from, where scientists from Laboratoire Garnier and Clinique do their work. Science fiction doesn't think of scientists manufacturing eyeliner, but it's all state-of-design manufacturing. Chemicals escape from the lab as products, and then migrate across the surface of women, and women steer this process along rather than resisting. Women always say yes to mutation. In the morning, I'll look like this, and in the evening,*

I'll look like this. Women are inside mutation, inside change from an early age, rather than finding a real self that you hold against change. That's why women make good science-fiction characters.

WG: I agree. In the unspoken tradition of American science fiction that I felt I was writing against, even having a female character who thought about makeup was a wonderful violation, completely transgressed the whole culture. Imagine writing a book with no women at all. Urgghh.

KE: *Manuel DeLanda — this chaos theorist argues that if you trip you change your brain from a solid state to a liquid state. The brain becomes this liquid computer, and you can process far more information than you would normally. As soon as you do that, then you can start to think of technology as the secret life of machines. You want to get at the abstract workings of the machine; what the machines think of you rather than what the operators thought they were doing with machines. What do today's machines think of us? In your books bikes snarl, fridges beseech, cars have attitude. There are all these transfers of power to machines.*

The Difference Engine is definitely the book in which the machine attains artificial intelligence because it turns out to be the narrator, although you never realize this until the very end.

WG: If you're rewriting with another person, it takes over, and it becomes a form of time travel. There was no Internet then. We wound up exchanging discs. By the end there was this literary synaesthesia. The last twenty pages of the book really did seem to emerge from some other, from some third mind. It delighted us, but it also chilled us both because it's much, much darker than either of us had really anticipated; really very dystopian. We were taking dictation from the active voice of the book that literally turned out to be this computer.

KE: *The computer was using you to run its operating systems.*

WG: When it became evident that the artificial intelligence posed by the book was in fact writing the book, that was the central conceit, and that voice would take over, and you would hear it by the end of the book; you would experience that voice directly. Neither of us expected the voice when it emerged. By that time I had a fax machine, I saw the end of that come scrolling out of my brand-new fax machine.

KE: *Is that because the book opens up a nonhuman emergence which lies somewhere between superseding the human and a new co-evolutionary arrangement in which humans have to share control?*

WG: It felt like we had created our own artificial intelligence. There's this famous parapsychology experiment where people deliberately try and create a ghost. It's like they're doing a séance in reverse. There is no ghost. The room's not haunted, but they managed to get these effects. The table moves. That's what it felt like we were doing. Between the two of us, we dreamed an artificial intelligence and managed to frighten ourselves with it. The voice that emerged at the end was colder and stranger than anything either of us could have separately.

KE: *What did the scientists conclude about inventing a ghost?*

WG: The conclusion is that there are rational but extremely strange mechanisms, non-supernatural mechanisms to account for séance behavior. There's much more going in the group mind than Victorian science could comprehend.

KE: *The walkie talkie ticks and whispers, the bike barks at you to back off, the fridge suggests a snack: technology talks back to you with various levels of intelligence. If there's going to be artificial intelligence, it will most likely evolve in ways least likely to be human. People wouldn't recognize it for what it is. At what stage of evolution is machine intelligence at now and is it adapting us every step of the way?*

WG: I think it's more that we'll become more like our machines, rather than vice versa. I suspect that the fact that we still bother to distinguish the one from the other is one of the things that would most date, from the viewpoint of future generations.

KE: *Today it's the cyber-feminist Sadie Plant who has real insights into co-evolution. She argues about corporations: "People may think they're running the whole show, but they're just tiny components subject to the same sort of molecular engineering as the rest of us, and what they think they are doing in the context of emergent planetary intelligence is irrelevant to what they are actually doing. There's a big split all the way between intentions and effects." Is this your sense of events?*

WG: Intelligent aliens studying us from a distance might well assume that multinational corporations are the most evolved lifeform on our planet. They transcend both the individual and the state. [Looks away momentarily to point up at the back garden through window.] Wow, talk about light. Look at the light on the top of that Douglas Fir out there. Look at those pinecones. Lord. In another month those'll all be down.

KE: *At one point Virtual Reality was the cutting edge of technology. Why does it now look so clunky and so corny? Was this clunkiness there from the start or is it the side effect of a future that just never arrived?*

WG: The popular media image of VR, the pretty girl in the goggles and gloves, definitely feels nostalgic now. I've been saying for a few years now that goggles-and-gloves VR is starting to feel awfully long in the tooth. It's starting to feel like the flying car that they promised our parents after the war. It's become a nostalgic image. But I think it's initial popularity stemmed from it having been such a brilliant, if thoroughly unconscious visual metaphor for what we already do with media. A very poignant icon.

KE: *Let's take the Oncomouse as an evolutionary intelligence. When I first saw the Oncomouse with the ear growing out of it's back I became obsessed because I wanted to know what it could hear. I still want to know what that ear growing out of it's back, that strange pink ear, can hear. I really want to know. I look at that ear, and I feel really strange. You know in the nineteenth century you had that His Master's Voice dog looking at the gramophone with its big ear trumpet. When I look at the mouse I feel like that dog. [I howl in sympathy.]*

WG: [Laughs loudly.]

KE: *That ear! What is it hearing? It's a big fleshy umbrella, a fleshy satellite dish transmitting and receiving information. Who knows, who can ask it? In the presence of that ear I'm just reduced and dumbfounded. Today, technology's role is to expand the realm of the riddle, the unknown. Previously, I think people thought science's role was to clarify, elucidate, enlighten, and make everything legible. But science fills the world with inscrutable machines. Who knows what that phone thinks of us as it sits there? Technology expands the area of mythology rather than clarifies it. When I see the Oncomouse I can't really take any art seriously anymore. I don't even know the name of the scientists who engineered it. They're anonymous geneticists just like trainer designers, but, to me, these people are the true artists of our decade because they've superseded everything an artist could try to do. What did you think when you first saw the Oncomouse?*

WG: I wish that Marcel Duchamp could have seen it. [Laughs.] It's so classically surreal, I can't imagine what Duchamp or Picabia would have made of the Oncomouse.

KE: *It makes me feel like I'm at the beginning of the century and I know nothing. I might as well be in the seventeenth century. All your knowledge disintegrates in the face of it. The mouse looks so baffled and oblivious. In the first satellite, you had Laika the dog. Animals are always the advance guards; they are literally the avant-garde in the front of technological evolution so it's quite obvious that if you look at that mouse that's what in store for us. [Laughs.] It's a microcosm of future human adaptation. In the next fifteen years, you'll be able to grow third ears on demand, and I look forward to it. You were just saying how VR is a nostalgic technology for you now.*

WG: Yeah, yeah, it's very '80s.

KE: What about nanotechnology in *Idoru*?

WG: I've never been able to get my head around nanotech. I use it in an almost ironic way. I like the effect of another level of apocalyptic technological change looming in the background.

KE: *In* Idoru, *you destroy Tokyo and then nanotechnically rebuild it. When Laney looks out of the window at night he can see buildings growing themselves. This fascinates me because it's biology of architecture. When Laney sees buildings grow themselves, there's the move into a new nature, biology of the city. It's like seeing an urban version of those nature films where a flower speeds up very fast.*

WG: So far I've used nanotechnology as a kind of incomprehensible next threshold of stuff. Whenever I've listened to any of the pro-nanotech people around Drexler, I'm reduced to tears of laughter. What they're talking about is so completely unimaginable. If they can make that stuff work, it will change things so totally that everything that's gone before it in terms of technology will just seem like nothing at all. It's like a black hole. Everything will go down it, and you'll be on the other side in this incomprehensible posthuman space, so I use it in *Virtual Light* and *Idoru* at its most ironic. But more frequently, just in the last couple of months, there's been more and more nanotech news. Yesterday, someone faxed me an article about flexible semi-conductors, which people in the States have come up with. This is how science-fiction writers exchange ideas. How about this for a very Sterling thing. I thought it was very funny. [Goes to fax machine. Tears off page after page.] Reads: "All bets are off! They bend like rubber!" [Laughs.]

KE: *Reads: "New flexible semiconductors which can be peeled right off their substrates" discovered by a group of Buffalo physicists.*

WG: Just what that suggests. You know the rollup computer. And what you could do with clothing. You could build winter jackets with whole mainframes inside them. Peel them off like bumper stickers. Peel them off the backing and stick them on. There's a constant stream of this stuff but just in the last couple of months there's being more and more functional nanotech.

KE: *I read a piece by R.U. Sirius in* Artforum *where he suggested that most people's response to the new is one of total and unbridled cynicism, 110-degrees of cynicism. But some level of nanotech, he reckons, will happen and science fiction is doing what it always does. It's rehearsing your perception of events about to take place. Whenever a science fiction writer extrapolates forward from a particular technological system, they're acting as futureshock absorbers. Science fiction cushions you against an inevitably traumatizing experience, which is just round the corner. Every year, more breakthroughs get made which are bound to reach a point of singularity at which point we cross a threshold, we're in another age from which there's no turning back. It's at this point that people immediately look back to the age that's just become irrelevant to get them through. So things should proceed the other way around. Before we get to the Nano Age, we should look to the guides that conceptually predetermine what might happen. Ballard used to say the future is a better guide to the present than the past. In other words science fiction registers the anxieties of nanotech better than traditional science. The weird thing is, no one in your Tokyo ever talks about it.*

WG: [Laughs.]

KE: *At its best, science fiction delivers shocks to the system, lights up the sensorium with new human machine interfaces. But what if simultaneously it's immersing you in the destructive element. Nanotech is undoubtedly one of the traumas to come, so let's acclimatize ourselves to it. Going forward to Ballard again, the coolest thing he did was to conceptualize new catastrophes for just this reason. Unlike Japan, England's got no tradition of catastrophe movies. It would do people a world of good to see their most familiar landscapes being systematically destroyed. I was watching* Independence Day, *and I thought how enjoyable to see New York City going up in flames, to hear the White House pluming and cracking.*

WG: Yeah. It's extremely cathartic.

KE: *Ballard says the catastrophic novel is an extremely positive act on behalf of the novelist. It's an attempt to impeach the universe, to indict time and space for their terminal indifference. Japanese disaster movies have been mercilessly destroying cities since the '50s.*

WG: They were assumed to be doing that in the wake of Hiroshima. And yet there was never any equivalent in the UK. If the Battle of Britain was seen as a triumph, then all the bombing couldn't be there in the unconscious in the same way so you got *Day of the Triffids* instead of the British Godzilla knocking down Big Ben which would have been great. In Berlin, there's this huge stump of this enormous cathedral that they've left in the center of town as an anti-war monument. So it's just this stump that towers over everything, and you think about the explosive power required to reduce something like that to a little nub. It's an impressive war monument. But science fiction is getting off to a slow start in nanotech terms. There's only been a handful of nanotech novels. Greg Bear's wonderfully weird *Blood Music* is still the one people remember.

KE: *If the future's inevitably traumatising, then maybe SF isn't just an early warning device. Maybe it's a buffer zone.*

WG: Buffer zone in a sense where you can teach people to play with alternative possibilities. Maybe that works better in theory than in practice, given that the majority of science fiction is oddly reactionary.

KE: *And boring. An hour not spent reading it is an hour saved forever. We always go for the books with your blurbs on them, William.*

WG: Well this is dangerous, this is dangerous.

KE: *Why do you say that?*

WG: Well, there are blurbs, and then there are blurbs. You cannot always believe all of everyone's blurbs.

KE: *[Laughs.]*

WG: You have to judge the level of enthusiasm. [Laughs.] I know I've blurbed a few things in my day.

KE: *Let's talk about the* Idoru *in the novel, Rei. This is modelled on Japanese, girl popstars.*

WG: Well, I ran across this story in Karl Taro Greenfield's *Speed Tribes,* which is a wonderful book about contemporary Japanese pop culture. I ran across this story of an *Idoru* who didn't actually exist. They hadn't bothered to have a girl. They just do the publicity, have the photograph, and have someone else sing and she became very popular. Toward the end of her career, she was doing things like publishing books of poetry and shows of her watercolors. That seemed so funny and resonant. Because I often think, what if a celebrity you believed in didn't exist? What if you realized one day that there really wasn't any Arnold Schwarzenegger? So I started playing with that and came up with Rei. Subsequently after turning in the manuscript, I discovered that there are virtual *Idoru* on a large level in Japan.

KE: *You hit on another nodal point then.*

WG: Yeah. There's an *Idoru* called Kyoku Bate in Tokyo, and I've been to her website and downloaded her rather startling image. She's a non-existent, Japanese girl who supposedly was going to release her first single in August, but it doesn't seem to have come out. I'm doing a Q&A with her, and I ask her what her blood type is. I ask her all the things Japanese journalists ask me.

KE: *Japanese journalists ask about your bloodtype?*

WG: Yeah. There's a very odd belief in Japan sort of like astrology that blood type determines personality. This is based on a single completely wacky best-selling book in the '80s that came with a do-it-yourself blood-testing kit. You could find out right there which type you were and then read about what your characteristics would be. The first interview I did in Japan, the guy said, "What is your blood type?"

KE: *Did you know?*

WG: No. Do you think that today's technology and science is going to make the avant-garde sort of impossibility?

KE: *Yeah. I tend to think of the avant-garde as a holding pen. Artists always want to deterritorialize things while the avant-garde is this critical institution that locks things down. I think the pop art of music rescues gallery bound art from its avant-garde prison, gets it out of jail. Art's admirers, i.e., its critics, bestow an avant-garde status on art out of love, which calcifies, solidifies, petrifies any movement that art might have. Admirers put the brakes on breaks. A good art form should be a break/flow machine: it should break with things and simultaneously generate a new flow between things. But people who really, really admire these arts come along and freeze them. The avant-garde was a nineteenth-century French military term for the frontline, the soldiers who took the first bullets. It's a suicidal term but it won't go away because it's* *so built into knowledge economies it's like a phantom limb. People insist on it even though it's—*

WG: [Laughs.]

KE: *—long gone. They feel the avant-garde like a phantom limb. It just hangs there uselessly. To this day people refer to the avant-garde like it has a specifiable meaning we can all agree on.*

WG: Yeah that's true. The phantom limb of the avant-garde. I like that very much.

KE: *It's not really on anymore. The confusion of this moment is much better. In my book on the intersection of science fiction and sound which I call "sonic fiction" or "phono fiction," all these tired terms, postmodern, modern, avant-garde have been replaced with remixology, sampladelia, conceptoxin which is any concept that makes you ill like ideology, critique, representation, the other. Universities are very good at giving you conceptoxins. Possibly all education is nothing but an imbibing of conceptoxins. All philosophy is anyway because thought is entirely delibidinized. Thought has no smell, no taste. It's not biological.*

WG: [Laughs.]

KE: *This abstraction process: elevated up into your head then past your head into the clouds and you're a real thinker. But it's the opposite. You need your hands to interface, your fingers for the trackball, for the keyboards. In* Idoru *your characters are always clicking, pointing, thumbing, a whole series of manual operations other than typing.*

WG: It's a really physical thing.

KE: *You once suggested that the destiny of technology was to get closer to the skin, more flush. Instead of distancing itself from the body, technology's drive is towards greater and greater tactility. We can follow this in derms and micropores, but where after this?*

WG: I like Eno's idea of the "African" computer, the interface you wear, dance with/in.

KE: *It's dermal thought, embodied knowledge. In the Trilogy, there's a lot of derms. I remember reading about Nicorette patches for smokers and being startled that they'd arrived.*

WG: I was looking at a magazine for HIV-positive people, and there was a full-page ad for testosterone derms because in some stages of HIV, you can suffer from a lowering of testosterone. I thought, "my God! What could you do with testosterone derms?" [Chuckles.] Just the street use, you know. Slap one of these babies on and get ready for a rocky Friday night. [Laughs.]

KE: *I remember a line in your fiction about the queasy feeling of "the rotten pharmacological scaffolding" collapsing in your stomach as the drug takes hold.*

WG: [Laughs.]

KE: *This is very precise because although people say "she's off her head" you don't feel out of your head, you feel in your body, you feel the peristaltic motion.*

WG: They put you further into your body. Styles change. [Laughs.] Fashions in drug use change, but I'm sure we've only sampled a tiny fragment of the possible pharmacopoeia. If you read Shulgin's book, *Phikal,* some of those ones that he just says, "hmmm, I don't think I'll do this again"; [laughs] you wonder what that one was like. He's apparently being shut down. He used to have some sort of license to experiment with those things but apparently no more. I think the publication of that book had a lot to do with it. If you knew enough about chemistry you could manufacture those molecular arrangements. I don't think those things are that easy to make. I think you can tell by the variation in the quality of ecstasy that it's not that easy to make.

KE: *People are a lot poorer in London than in Europe. There's a lower standard of living than here or the States. No one has much money and drugs simultaneously anaesthetize and open you up to experience and before you know it there's a music that's feeds it and once there's a drug/technology feedback cycle there's a rollercoaster which sustains itself. People get locked into the ongoing toxic drive. Nobody wants lyrics or messages.*

WG: It's a completely different landscape there. I think that is the difference. Verbal information: no! [Laughs.] You know the reason why I think you've got that? The reason why I think that's happening in England and Europe for the past decade at least is that you've had a working drug culture. You've had a drug culture that produces music. There's a feedback loop that's always changing. That hasn't been happening here for a long time. There are drugs, but there's not a drug culture, not in the same way. [Laughs.] All the same post-amphetamine drugs that brought that on in Europe and England never really happened here. They were just novelty drugs. Ecstasy's never been a distinctive thing except as an imitation of England. The drug that the Feds say is the most dangerous drug, which is always an interesting indication of something, is crystal meth in increasingly pure forms, like someone's found a way to make stronger crystals than we've ever had, and it's dirt cheap, and it's all down the West Coast, and it produced something called speed metal. It's just really hard, really fast for hours on end. The people who spent all that time putting those extra tails and curlicues on the methedrine molecules so that you could have ecstasy, what must they think?

KE: *You get this aversion to the verbal and this massive investment in the tonal. There's this idea that sound, rhythm can synthesize new emotions for you, that if you hear a sound you've never heard before then that's generating a new sensation. Emotion is a series* *of frequencies. It's the idea that you can manufacture new emotional states.*

WG: That's really interesting.

KE: *People go "I heard this new track," and, by implication, they felt a new feeling. It's the idea that these nonverbal states can travel across Europe via records, which are alien imports. The record releases an emotional current and it's up to you to transmit this tonal communication, pass it on. There's this amazing techno unit in Detroit called Underground Resistance, and all their records are installments in an ongoing audio-visual war against the programmers. Tonal communication happens outside the visual register. All mainstream music in the US goes through MTV, but Detroit Techno is this invisible music. Detroit Techno has seceded from America. They've internally emigrated from America.*

WG: Detroit's not there. Detroit's gone. Detroit's the only city in the United States where the downtown core of early twentieth-century skyscrapers are completely decimated and falling apart. There's actually a proposal to preserve the core of Detroit as the American Acropolis, as a beautiful ruin, and, of course, the people of Detroit aren't happy about this, but I thought it was a wonderful idea. Detroit has been in *Blade Runner* territory for twenty-five, thirty years and maybe that's why techno emerged from there. Techno is very, very neurospecific, I think. Otherwise people think it's dance music, and I don't dance.

KE: *It's very tense, anempathetic music a lot of the time. It impedes your normal strategies of investment, blocks your feelings. Even the idea of dance music is misunderstood in America. People don't yet understand that dance music operates on a new idea of the body as a big brain, a distributed brain. All of the body thinks. Music adapts your body so there's all these different kinds of bodily thought: dermal thought, hipthought, spinal thought, arsethought. If you're not used to them you won't even recognize the languages your body's operating on. Plus every society grades the body: the ass is probably shameful because that's where people shit from; the eyes are where the soul shines from. People will always mistake dance music for mindless music. But that's Cartesian, it's sixteenth century. Actually it's mind-full.*

WG: House music is a very neuroelectronically specific artifact. The dancers do indeed become part of an extended system, a system that uses technology to bridge the mind-body split in Western culture.

KE: *At the same time as your hackers were jacking into cyberspace in the Sprawl trilogy, Chicago house producers also began to talk about jacking your body, about getting inside the House that Jack built. To be inside the House that Jack built means you feel at home inside the machine, secure inside the beat. Dance music, futurhythmachine music opens up a human-machine intimacy that has no parallel in rock. What you really gain is the idea of the body as a distributed brain, a biocomputer of endless levels. Drugs can give you this sense of the body as this planet that we've only just landed on. In England, people are quite technologically backward. The net has taken off within media and college sectors, but it hasn't really penetrated to the extent that it has here. Here, there's a powerful sense that online technology leads to disembodiment while in England, because chemical/sonic technologies play the role that the net does here, the drive is much more toward reembodiment, forward into the levels of the biocomputer. The UK and the US are going very different ways.*

WG: I've always found it a bit puzzling, the ease with which that's been accepted because I never felt that I put it forward as anything more than a problematic aspect of the technology. But immediately after *Neuromancer* was published, I started encountering people who, somewhat to my dismay, completely identified with Case's rejection of the body, which had not been my intention at all. I'm inclined to think that the ease with which America accepts disembodiment has its roots in Calvinism. There's this puritan aspect that never really goes away. It's never been comfortable with the body in sensual ways, more so after the '60s. It's easy to forget historically the impact of psychedelia. Our whole range of colors has changed. The world would be very beige without it.

KE: *What do you think about your own fans?*

WG: Well you know I started putting up my own website a year ago, and, as we were putting it up, I realized there were already six or seven really elaborate websites put up by fans.

KE: *Any good?*

WG: Yeah, some of them are really great. If you wanted really straightforward information, it would be much better to go to those. My own is much more eccentric.

KE: *What are you putting up there?*

WG: Let's see. It's very graphics-intensive, so it's more like a design experience. There's images from a guy in the South who made porcelain dolls that you could buy. After he died they bulldozed his house and they found underneath it coffins filled with porcelain dolls of the neighborhood children. They recognized Jimmy Sue from down the street and Willie Mae, the one that looks Huck Finn-ish. They were in these harmless poses, but they were in coffins. We've got texts of talks I've given that otherwise wouldn't appear anywhere else and an autointerview in which I explain why I don't have an e-mail address.

KE: *You still don't have an e-mail address?*

WG: No, I still don't have an e-mail address. You can email this website, but you just get somebody that emails you right back saying he's not here. Sorry about that.

KE: This is your own version of an information diet or a media fast where you're controlling the input.

WG: Well yeah, I'm just terrible at answering mail. I would just have a ton of unanswered e-mail, and I don't know if it's that healthy to hear directly from one's audience. Every time I look at alt.cyberpunk I'm sure it will outlast me. [Sighs.] "Gibson has lost his edge." [Laughs.]

www.ingramcontent.com/pod-product-compliance
Lightning Source LLC
Chambersburg PA
CBHW072040160426
43197CB00014B/2565